# Praise for *Yes to the Mess*

"Finally! A book that applies the tools of an improvising jazz musician to great leadership. The modern world can no longer afford the orchestral model of management—lots of people playing the same part and a leader who stands apart from it all. The new world is premised on intense communication, lightning-speed decision making, risk taking, and a degree of perfected competence that allows spontaneous and brilliant composing—namely jazz. *Yes to the Mess* gets it right."

> —**Roger H. Brown**, President, Berklee College of Music;
> cofounder, Bright Horizons

"With the velvety tones of Wes Montgomery and the wail of Miles Davis, professional jazz musician and management scholar Frank Barrett plays a set to enchant us. Pour a glass of wine, sit back, and listen to this engaging story of how to help teams and organizations innovate instead of replicate."

> —**Richard Boyatzis**, Distinguished University Professor,
> Case Western Reserve University; coauthor,
> *Primal Leadership* and *Resonant Leadership*

"I've known Frank Barrett for over thirty years, and we've often discussed the strange confluence of learned experience and pure intuition that exists in jazz improvisation. Frank gives us an insight into that world and how its lessons can be applied to almost any walk of life—truly fascinating!"

> —**Ken Peplowski**, jazz musician

# YES TO THE MESS

# YES
# TO
# THE
# MESS

## Surprising Leadership Lessons from Jazz

# Frank J. Barrett

HARVARD BUSINESS REVIEW PRESS

BOSTON, MASSACHUSETTS

Library of Congress Cataloging-in-Publication Data

Barrett, Frank.
 Yes to the mess : surprising leadership lessons from jazz / Frank Barrett.
    p. cm.
 ISBN 978-1-4221-6110-4 (alk. paper)
 1. Leadership. 2. Creative ability. I. Title.
 HD57.7.B37 2012
 658.4'092–dc23

                                                                    2012013504

The paper used in this publication meets the requirements of the American National Standard for Permanence of Paper for Publications and Documents in Libraries and Archives Z39.48-1992.

This book is dedicated to two people.

First to my mother, Mary Hagan Barrett, who listened to me practicing the piano for years, witnessed me suffering through several clunkers, miscalculations, and wanderings (musical and otherwise), but always saw my potential better than I could myself. She is still the most resilient person I have ever known and has modeled what it means to continually say "yes."

This book is also dedicated to my late friend, mentor, and colleague, W. Barnett Pearce. Barnett was a continual source of friendship, inspiration, and good humor. I wish he were here to hold this book in his hands and see how his influence continues to grow.

# CONTENTS

Preface                                                                              ix

Acknowledgments                                                                     xvii

1  **All That Jazz**                                                                   1
   Mastering the Art of Unlearning

2  **"Yes to the Mess"**                                                             21
   Developing Affirmative Competence

3  **Performing and Experimenting Simultaneously**                                  41
   Embracing Errors as a Source of Learning

4  **Minimal Structure—Maximal Autonomy**                                           67
   Balancing Freedom and Constraints

5  **Jamming and Hanging Out**                                                       93
   Learning by Doing and Talking

6  **Taking Turns Soloing and Supporting**                                         119
   Followership as a Noble Calling

7  **Leadership as Provocative Competence**                                        135
   Nurturing Double Vision

8  **Getting to "Yes to the Mess"**                                                161
   Advancing Engaged, Strategic Improvisation

Notes                                                                              185

Index                                                                              193

About the Author                                                                   201

# PREFACE

*I wake to sleep, and take my waking slow.*
*I learn by going where I have to go.*
                    —Theodore Roethke, "The Waking"

On the surface this is a book about jazz improvisation. But relatively few of you who are reading these words are musicians, and many may not even like jazz music—although I hope that one consequence (not entirely unintended) of reading this book will be a deeper appreciation of jazz. This is really a book about the leadership mind-set and the kinds of activities and skills that help leaders understand and facilitate the innovation process.[1]

My own path may seem improvisational, or accidental. In the late 1980s when I was a graduate student in Organizational Behavior at Case Western Reserve University, I was at a conference where my dissertation advisor, Suresh Srivastva, introduced me to Karl Weick as "the doctoral student who used to play jazz." I remember two things from this encounter. First, I couldn't believe that I was really standing in front of, let alone talking to, Karl Weick. I and my fellow graduate students held his ideas in the highest esteem, and he had achieved, in our minds, pantheon status. The second thing I remember is what Karl said to me after Suresh told him of my former career as a jazz musician. Karl asked "Are you writing your dissertation about jazz as an innovative organization?" I mumbled an answer I don't recall now, but I remember thinking "Huh? What does jazz improvisation have to do with organizational behavior?" In fact I was well into my dissertation at the time and would graduate soon after, but Karl's question continued to echo, and I eventually began to see the connection that now seems so obvious. In the words of Theodore Roethke cited above, I was waking slowly.

I became increasingly intrigued with exploring the connection between my two passions—jazz and organizational behavior. In August 1995 at the Academy of Management in Vancouver, British Columbia, I partnered with Mary Jo Hatch to design and facilitate a lecture session and panel discussion on Jazz Improvisation and Organizational Complexity. Karl Weick was part of that panel. The papers that I and other participants wrote for this session were published in a special issue of *Organization Science* that appeared in 1998. Both the Vancouver session and the special journal issue further seeded my interest in the topic of improvisation in organizations. I began to draw upon the metaphor of jazz improvisation as a way to understand creativity and innovation, and developed executive education modules using improvisation as a lens for understanding collaborative innovation and organizational learning. I was surprised how much interest it generated.

This growing awareness and interest finally led me to write this book. I began to appreciate what a rich metaphor the jazz model is for understanding the nature of activity in organizations. I also began to see how the challenge of playing jazz is close to the challenges that executives face. In time, I realized that jazz is more than a metaphor for organizing. Jazz bands actually *are* organizations designed for innovation, and the design elements from jazz can be applied to other organizations seeking to innovate. Further, in order for jazz bands to be successful, they require a commitment to a mind-set, a culture, practices and structures, and a leadership framework that is strikingly similar to what it takes to foster innovation in organizations.

In this book I use jazz improvisation as a touch point to outline seven principles that are a supporting framework for understanding how to nurture strategic improvisation and innovation. These seven principles became the book's chapter titles. In each chapter I alternate between jazz illustrations and stories of organizations, with an eye toward showing how these principles are already in practice in many organizations and how leaders can support and expand opportunities for innovation. My hope is that executives will glean useful insights about the choices and activities that jazz improvisers make, preparing to be spontaneous and balancing between constraints and experimentation in public performance. Leaders would do well to consider these seven principles and use these insights to create a culture of innovation that encourages engaged and strategic improvisation.

The first principle, "All That Jazz: Mastering the Art of Unlearning" (chapter 1), is a call to guard against the seductive power of routines. Often the first step to gaining the new insight necessary for innovation is to unlearn. There is a human tendency, especially in established organizations, to rely upon well-worn routines and familiar rules. Over time, the way things are usually done becomes sacred and unquestioned. These routines are blocks to learning. Because of the temptation to repeat what they do well rather than risk failure, veteran jazz musicians make deliberate attempts to guard against the reliance on prearranged music, memorized solos, or habits and patterns that have worked for them in the past. Instead, they challenge themselves to explore the very edge of their comfort level, to stretch their learning into new and different areas. Companies could stand to take a page from the jazz playbook. When organizations become locked in a dominant design, people find themselves trapped in roles, and dynamism is lost. This chapter raises the question: How can leaders do what jazz musicians do, deliberately disrupting routines as a way of "unlearning" so as to be more alive, alert, and open to a horizon of new possibilities?

The second principle, "'Yes to the Mess': Developing Affirmative Competence," is the subject of chapter 2. Managers frequently find themselves in the middle of messes not of their own making, in over their heads, having to take action even though there is no guarantee of a good outcome, and relying on imperfect information. Jazz players face the same issues, but what makes it possible to improvise, to adjust and fall upon a working strategy is an affirmative move, an implicit "yes" that allows them to move forward even in the midst of uncertainty. Problem solving by itself will not generate novel solutions. What's needed is an affirmative belief that a solution exists and that something positive will emerge. In fact this is a skill of the imagination, the capacity to suspend disbelief and leap into action with no objectively valid guarantee where one's actions will lead. Human beings are at their best when they are open to the world, able to notice what's needed, and equipped with the skills to respond meaningfully in the moment. Improvisation grows out of a receptivity to what the situation offers and thus the first move is a "yes to the mess," a state of radical receptivity that all jazz musicians yearn toward.

The third principle, "Performing and Experimenting Simultaneously: Embracing Errors as a Source of Learning" (chapter 3), discusses the importance of creating a culture of learning. Leaders need to do what jazz musicians do—anticipate that when people are encouraged to try something new, the results will be unexpected, and "unexpectable," including errors. Innovative cultures maximize learning by nurturing a mind-set of enlightened trial and error that allows managers to take advantage of errors to offer new insights. This involves creating a psychological comfort zone, one in which it is safe for people to talk about errors and what can be learned from them. Such a culture doesn't pretend that errors never happen. Nor does it punish them excessively. Rather, it embraces failures as occasions for learning.

The next principle is "Minimal Structure—Maximal Autonomy: Balancing Freedom and Constraints" (chapter 4). This principle fosters a flexible structure—an organizational design that has both sufficient constraints, just enough structure and coordination to maximize diversity. Jazz bands and innovative organizations create the conditions for guided autonomy. They create choice points to avoid getting weighted down with fruitless rules while also maximizing diversity, inviting embellishment, and encouraging exploration and experimentation. To foster innovation, leaders hedge against the trap of "too much consensus," giving people freedom to experiment and respond to hunches. The underlying assumption is that when two people disagree, they're both right. Thus, such organizations tolerate and encourage dissent and debate.

The fifth principle, "Jamming and Hanging Out: Learning by Doing and Talking," is taken up in chapter 5. In jazz, learning and ideas for innovation take place in jam sessions, the creative equivalent of conversations in nineteenth-century coffeehouses. It is here that musicians get innovative ideas and learn how and whether their playing is up to par. For rookies and semi-outsiders, these sessions are where they learn what it takes to think and act like a jazz insider. Organizations need to create similar room for jam sessions, as Steve Jobs so deeply understood. They need to deliberately design for serendipity, to encourage happy accidents and unexpected discoveries. The key to this in organizations is *opportunistic conversations*. Great insights occur in the context of relationships and exchanges, as people share each other's work and ask questions (often naïve questions).

The sixth principle is "Taking Turns Soloing and Supporting: Followership as a Noble Calling" (chapter 6). We put so much emphasis on leadership today that we have forgotten the importance of followership, what jazz musicians call "comping." In organizations, followership—supporting others to think out loud and be their best—should be an art more fully articulated, acknowledged, and rewarded. This chapter urges leaders to model and support the importance of taking turns as leaders and supporters, just as great jazz leaders do. Followership can be a noble calling, and organizations need to let it flourish.

The seventh principle is "Leadership as Provocative Competence: Nurturing Double Vision" (chapter 7). Provocative competence is a very special leadership skill that helps people break out of competency traps. Practicing provocative competence requires first that leaders discipline their imaginations to see a person's or group's potential even if it is not being fulfilled in that moment. Leaders can introduce an incremental disruption that demands that people leave their comfort zones and attempt new and unfamiliar actions. In effect, leaders are provoking "learning vulnerability"—moments of disquiet (and excitement) in which people are exploring the unfamiliar. Finally, provocative competence involves facilitating a reorientation. Duke Ellington and Miles Davis were masters of provocative competence;

they understood that it was an art form in itself. Leaders in every sector would do well to heed the lesson.

Chapter 8 offers a summary and a look forward, an improvisation toolkit that offers concrete steps leaders can take to seed a culture that notices and values improvisation.

We have grown up with a variety of models of organizations, most of which have relied to some degree on a mechanistic view of top-down approaches to change. Command-and-control models of leadership stress routines and rules. They demand rigorous and clear organizational structures reinforced by rules, plans, budgets, PERT charts, schedules, clearly defined roles, and the use of coercion or intimidation to get worker compliance. These might have worked well in the first part of the twentieth century when organizations were designed like machines, tasks were broken down into small parts that could be easily replicated, and people could be replaced as easily as machine parts. But as we enter the knowledge-intensive demands of the twenty-first century, we need to rotate our images and increase our leadership repertoire beyond these hierarchical models, so that we more fully appreciate the power of relationships.

This new era demands focusing on teams rather than individuals, encouraging ongoing learning and innovation rather than compliance to preordained plans. Leaders don't have the luxury of anticipating or predicting every situation, training and rehearsing for it, and getting learning out of the way before executing. Rather, leaders must master the art of learning *while* doing and spread this mastery throughout their systems. That's why jazz bands are such provocative models for us to consider as we create teams and organizations in the twenty-first century.

How do organizations thrive in a drastically changing world predicated on uncertainty? By building a capacity to experiment, learn, and innovate—in short, by engaging in strategic, engaged improvisation. The model of jazz musicians improvising collectively offers a clear and powerful example of how people and teams can coordinate, be productive, and create amazing innovations without so many of the control levers that managers relied on in the industrial age. An improvisation model of organizing creates a kind of openness, an invitation to possibility, rather than leaning toward a narrowness of control.

This book is an invitation for leaders to take a robust approach to innovation, to create vital cultures that enhance discovery rather than falling into the narrow predictability of the known world. It's an invitation for leaders to break open some of the rigid conventions that they live within, to experience what it's like to leap beyond certitude. Saying "yes to the mess" challenges us all to create engaged, passionate, and imaginative cultures, communities, and organizations in helping the progress and well-being of the whole system.

Jazz musicians seek to live lives of radical receptivity. Human beings are at their best when they do the same—when they are open to the world, able to notice expansive horizons of possibility, fully engaged in skillful activity, and living in contexts that summon responses that lead to new discoveries. How can we organize so as to make it possible for people to be at their best? That is the question that guides the inquiry behind this book.

# ACKNOWLEDGMENTS

Thanks to my brainstorming friends and colleagues who have helped me clarify my thinking and offered insight and encouragement over the years—my deepest gratitude to Ken Gergen, Mary Gergen, Karl Scheibe, Sheila McNamee, the late Barnett Pearce, the late Ted Sarbin, Marc Ventresca, Ed Schein, David Cooperrider, Ronald Fry, Bill Pasmore, Richard Boyatzis, Karl Weick, Mary Jo Hatch, Richard Doyle, Jean Bartunek, Joe Rubel, Sarah Johnson, and Sonia Nevis.

I deeply value my two years as a Visiting Scholar at Harvard Business School and the Harvard Program on Negotiation. I especially thank my sponsors, Mike Wheeler and Amy Edmondson. It was at Harvard that I first envisioned and began working on this book. I had many seminal conversations with Mike, Amy, and others at HBS, especially Andreea Gorbatai, Dutch Leonard, Clay Christensen, Mike Tushman, Ethan Bernstein, and Colin Fisher. I am grateful, too, for the inspirational conversations I had with my friends and colleagues at Harvard Graduate School of Education and Harvard Faculty of Arts and Sciences, especially Richard Hackman, Bob Kegan, Monica Higgins, Laura Crandall, Lissa Young, Sean Kelly, Larry Susskind, Kim Leary, and Jane Juliano.

Thanks to my friends and colleagues who've read and commented on earlier versions of this manuscript—especially Ed Schein, Bill Van Buskirk, Marty Kaplan, Kyle Johnson, Ralph Carney, Richard Boyatzis, Herbert Anderson, Bill Pasmore, Michael Fish, and Karl Weick.

Thanks also to my colleagues at the Naval Postgraduate School who offered helpful comments and critiques on earlier drafts, especially Reuben Harris, Nick Dew, Wayne Porter, Nancy Roberts, Kishore Sengupta, Tarek Abdel-Hamid, Jim Suchan, and David Franta.

To my friends and colleagues at Fielding Graduate University, especially Jeremy Shapiro, Mike Manning, Charlie Seashore, Charles

McClintock, Judy Stevens-Long, Pamela Meyer, and Cate Creede—thank you for working to keep me humble. I'm trying.

A very special thanks to Mike Wheeler from Harvard Business School. Mike's friendship and support have been invaluable. He saw the potential for this book before I did and continued to remind me of its potential, especially in those moments when I was losing sight of my goal. For Mike, friendship is a highly developed art, and he practices it with craftsmanlike skill. Chapter 6 is about the role of "comping," supporting others to do their best work. It is dedicated to Mike.

Thanks to those who helped me get these ideas from proposal to manuscript—Rafe Sagalyn and Shannon O'Neill. Thanks also for the wonderful editing of Howard Means, who kept me from hiding behind academic clichés, helped me develop a practitioner's voice, and provided much-needed clarity on several occasions.

Thanks to the staff at Harvard Business Review Press and especially my editor, Jeff Kehoe, for his appreciative eye (and musical ear) and for advising me from the earliest stages to help move this project forward. I have enjoyed our partnership and look forward to further opportunities to collaborate.

Thanks to my family and friends for encouraging me and for being understanding, especially during those times when I wasn't available and not in the best of moods.

Thanks especially to my friends who've come to understand the challenges of being an introvert who's occasionally thrust into public roles. I'm trying to get better. Thanks for your patience.

A special thanks to Doug Conant, recently retired CEO of Campbell Soup, who models what it means to be a leader devoted to helping others learn and develop.

I would like to thank my students, especially the officers at the Naval Postgraduate School. You have been, and continue to be, my teachers.

I'd like to thank all of those musicians who inspired me over the years. First and foremost I acknowledge the influence of my first mentor, the great ragtime pianist, Arthur E. Hagan—my grandfather. He showed me that you can lift the mood of any group (or family) with a good song. And if there's no piano on hand, a good sense of humor will suffice. I hope I can carry his influence forward.

I'd like to acknowledge all of those musicians who have devoted their lives to playing jazz. You have been called to a special profession, and I hope that you reap some of the blessings you bestow on your listeners. My earliest jazz inspirations—Oscar Peterson, Duke Ellington, Thelonius Monk, Bill Evans, Herbie Hancock, and Keith Jarrett—are deserving of my special thanks and acknowledgment. Later in this book I say some things that are critical of Oscar Peterson, but these remarks pale in comparison to my deep admiration for him and for his playing.

Thanks to those musicians with whom I've played over the years and who have sharpened my ear and improved my technique. There are simply too many to mention. In jazz, as in most things, I was a late bloomer; I didn't begin playing jazz until I was twenty-six. I must specifically acknowledge the first jazz musician I ever played with— Ken Peplowski. What a lucky moment that was. I had a few glimpses then of how fortunate I was to play with such a gifted musician who consistently pushed me to play beyond my capacity. Little did I know then that Ken was destined for such accomplishment. Most recently I've been honored to play with my friend and colleague Colin Fisher, assistant professor of management at Boston University. I look forward to many more collaborations with this gifted friend. To all those with whom I've shared the bandstand—thank you. These learning experiences have been joyous, occasionally transcendent, sometimes painful, always humbling, and the catalyst for my own reflections and theory building.

# YES
# TO
# THE MESS

## CHAPTER ONE

# All That Jazz

## Mastering the Art of Unlearning

Businesses have plans for everything: sales (in one-, three-, and five-year projections), mergers, acquisitions, R&D, doomsdays and glory days, and just about every eventuality in between. Indeed, the only plan that's missing, it often seems, is the one for things as they actually happen.

Let's take BP as an example. The British-based petroleum giant definitely had a plan for what to do if a wellhead blew in the Gulf of Mexico. In fact, it had two of them: a 582-page regional spill plan for the Gulf generally and a 52-page plan specific to the Deepwater Horizon site. But as became painfully evident in the weeks after the fatal April 20, 2010, explosion at the Deepwater rig, both plans were riddled with problems.

The regional response plan, for example, contained instructions on how to keep walruses from being affected by an oil spill—important to walruses, but a species unknown to such temperate waters. Among the go-to people the plan suggested calling was Miami sea-turtle expert Peter Lutz, but Lutz had changed location two decades earlier and was no longer reachable in any event—he had died in 2004.

Deepwater oil reached the Mississippi River delta in nine days, although BP's computer modeling had given it a one-in-five chance of getting there within a month, patchwork solutions serially failed, and BP's carefully cultivated image as a global petro "green giant" lay shredded on the Gulf seabed.

Rather than consulting the company's disaster playbook, then-CEO Tony Hayward and his fellow top executives might have done better heeding the advice of former heavyweight champion Mike Tyson. "Everyone," Tyson once said, "has a plan until they get punched in the mouth." This book is about building a mind-set for our complex, fast-moving world in which even the best-laid plans are likely, figuratively, and sometimes literally to get punched in the mouth.

The management guru Peter Drucker imagined the twenty-first-century business leader as an orchestra conductor who, following a prescripted score, coaxes great performances out of an orchestra not necessarily composed of great musicians. Adequate talent would do so long as the musicians produced at their peak after "rehearsing the same passage in the symphony again and again until the first clarinet plays it the way the conductor hears it."[1]

My admiration for Drucker is almost boundless, but I believe his conductor metaphor fails to account for the enormous ambiguity and turbulence in the current environment. I'm drawn instead to the model developed by Karl Weick in his influential paper, "Improvisation as a Mindset for Organizational Analysis."[2] As Weick argues, organizations consist of a group of diverse specialists who, under great duress, make fast, irreversible decisions, are highly interdependent, are dedicated to creation and novelty, and act with little certainty where it's all going to end up.

Surely that's the situation BP executives found themselves in after the Deepwater Horizon explosion: great duress with virtually no certainty where it would all come out in the end and, critically, accompanied by little comfort with or training for the enormous ambiguity that engulfed them. The stumbling, fumbling results speak for themselves, but just as surely, the heads of many different enterprises looked at the daily media circus swirling around BP and thought, there but for grace and blind luck go I.

This is the way things are today. Big goofs end up on YouTube, but even modest mistakes can go viral in hours and take months to overcome. Products and services are almost instantly replicable; competition is ferocious and likely to emerge from any point on the compass; and thus price points, margins, and market share evaporate overnight.

What are the models for surviving and prospering in such a climate? In medicine, not the relatively controlled and sterile environment of the operating room, but the sometimes frantic triage of a field hospital, where wounds and diseases are constantly novel, conditions are always at least slightly chaotic, and the outcome is wildly unpredictable. In football, not the near-infinite permutations and combinations on basic formations—the offensive guru Al Saunders can throw 700-plus different plays at an NFL defense—but the madcap, scrambling genius of a quarterback like Michael Vick, who prospers best when the protection breaks down, his receivers are all covered, and it's every man for himself. And in entertainment, not the prescribed and approved yuks of situation comedy but the often desperate lurches of stand-up comics at the local improv, where a really bad outing might actually bring on Mike Tyson's punch in the mouth.

Admittedly, my sense of comic timing is strained at best, and my gridiron days were never particularly pretty. As for surgery, I'm semi-competent at splinter removal, nothing more. But there is one improv field that I know about deep in my bones, and I happen to think it's the best model of all for business in the twenty-first century: that great American original art form known as jazz.

I come with a bias—I'm a jazz pianist. I have traveled the world with the Tommy Dorsey Band and led my own trios and quartets. I'm also a management professor, and it's safe to say I've learned as much about leadership and organizational behavior—and what it takes to excel as a performer—from my riffing at the piano as I have from my academic experience.

My piano training began, inauspiciously, with formal lessons at age eight. Try as I might to play, say, the B-flat minor scale with correct fingering—thumb crossing under, elbow tucked in tightly—I would repeatedly flub it. Eventually, the teacher told my mother to stop throwing good money after bad, and the lessons ended. But when I wasn't practicing rigid scales and chord productions, I found I could perform complicated duets with my grandfather, Arthur E. Hagan. He was a ragtime piano player and as a teenager had played the piano for silent movies in Cleveland theaters. For a fumbling, restless eight-year-old boy, my grandfather was a perfect teacher—kind, patient, and humorous. In fact, I taped some of those childhood sessions, and when I now listen to that schoolboy, syncopated version of "Bye Bye Blues," I hear a fairly advanced sense of time and rhythm, not to mention facility with the keys.

What was so different in my two styles of "practice"? Well, I learned boogie-woogie piano not by reading sheet music and practicing rote, but by mimicking my grandfather—the way he sat, his unusual footwork on the pedals, the runs and licks he played. Even when I couldn't hit the exact notes, I echoed his rhythms and gestures, and when I'd imitate his playing, even when I hit "clunker" notes, he would simply delight in my efforts. There was no such thing as a mistake. Unbeknownst to my young self, that mimicry was setting down the hardwiring that would later allow me to become a more than competent jazz musician.

My training in management was nowhere near so much fun as learning to play the piano—especially when I was mastering "Maple Leaf Rag" at my grandfather's elbow—but it contained many of the same elements: both formal education and imitation of mentors and wise old hands who were as sympathetic about my vocational clunker notes as my grandfather had been about my earlier piano ones.

Still, it took an "aha" moment early in my teaching career to show me just how interrelated the two pursuits are, or should be. Truth told, I wasn't much of a professor when I first started out. I knew exactly what lessons and insights I wanted my students to get. I devised tests and exams that reinforced my "truths," and I spared little effort in letting students know when they were getting it wrong.

Then one day a student interrupted me with a question that had nothing to do with the teaching plan, and out of exasperation—he was disrupting my plan after all—I said (and in memory, almost shouted), "Why are you asking that?" He answered honestly, "Because I'm curious." That stopped me in my tracks long enough to say to myself, "We want students to be curious. That's good. Maybe I should see where this leads." So I surrendered and let go of my plan. We started in on the question the student had raised, and thirty minutes later, I realized we had covered the original topic in a deeper, more creative way than I ever could have imagined. What's more, I saw how often I had been more loyal to my teaching plan than I was to the students and how, as a result, I had been blocking the learning process.

Before long, I was searching for moments when my students' grasp of a problem departed from mine, and pursuing their questions, not just my own. With that, my entire experience changed. Simply put, I began to love teaching the day I found out that I was also learning—perhaps more than the students. Students and teachers, I discovered, can be collaborative witnesses and catalysts. Together, we can bring new, unanticipated elements into the conversation, riffs that deepen our mutual experience and knowledge. These aren't teachable opportunities that can be planned for in advance. Rather, they are moments of learning that just happen along the way if—and "if" is the key word—we let them. And that for me was the real "aha" point of connection, because this is exactly what happens in jazz. The great moments are always the ones that happen along the way, if we let them.

In the years since, as I've honed the skills of my teaching profession and musical avocation, I have found more and more parallels between the dynamics in organizations, the tasks of leadership, and the improvisational nature of jazz. Moreover, I have come to see the powerful ways that jazz can help us in all our pursuits to be better leaders and innovators. The old models of organizations as command-and-control systems are outdated. We need a model of a group of diverse specialists living in a chaotic, turbulent environment; making fast, irreversible decisions; highly interdependent on one another to interpret imperfect and incomplete information; dedicated to innovation and the creation of novelty. This is what the great jazz players do: They learn by leaping in and taking action before they have a well-conceived plan. Once they've honed their skills, they know how to fabricate and invent novel responses without a scripted plan and no guarantee of outcomes. They discover the future as it unfolds. And they also discover their own identity—who they really are. Instead of dwelling on past mistakes, they take calculated risks and hope for the best, negotiating with each other as they proceed.

Except for a few scholars like Weick who have explored the improvisational mind-set in academic journals, no one has drawn on this model to explain how the principles of jazz can help anyone make the kinds of judgments and decisions required to perform at the top level in today's increasingly unpredictable organizations. That's what I do here. I urge readers to do as jazz players do: embrace the complexity of their lives, take informed risks, and finally, to borrow a phrase I use with my jazz-playing colleagues, "say yes to the mess."

## The Improv Paradox

The popular misconception is that jazz players are untutored geniuses who play their instruments as if they are picking notes out of thin air. But studies of jazz have shown that the art is very complex—*the result of a relentless pursuit of learning and disciplined imagination*. It's that relentless pursuit and disciplined imagination, not simple genius, that allow jazz players to improvise—from the Latin *improvisus*, meaning "not seen ahead of time"—and it's the improvisation that has become the defining hallmark of the art form.

How do jazz players learn to improvise? The same way I learned from my grandfather, the same way babies first learn to speak: by hearing patterns, watching gestures, and repeating and imitating. Jazz players build a vocabulary of phrases and patterns by imitating, repeating, and memorizing the solos and phrases of the masters until they become part of their repertoire of "licks."

There's irony here, of course. The goal of improvisation is to be mindful and creative, making up ideas on the spot that respond to what's happening in the moment, but the road to mindful adapting leads through copying and imitating because, as every jazz player learns, there are times when your only choice is to fall back on the patterns you learned through mindless habit.

Trumpeter Tommy Turrentine explains:

> *The old guys used to call those things crips. That's from crippled . . . In other words when you are playing a solo and your mind is crippled and you can't think of anything different to play, you go back into one of your old bags and play one of your crips. You better have something to play when you can't think of nothing new or you'll feel funny laying out there all the time.*[3]

After years of practicing and absorbing patterns, musicians recognize what phrases fit within different forms and the various options available within the constraints of specific chords and songs. They study other players' thought processes and learn to export materials from different contexts and vantage points, combining, extending, and varying the material, adding and changing notes, varying accents, subtly shifting the contour of a memorized phrase. Jazz critic Mark Gridley writes that Bill Evans was a master at this sort of highly cerebral improv:

> *Evans crafted his improvisations with exacting deliberation. Often he would take a phrase or just a kernel of its character, then develop and extend its rhythms, its melodic ideas, and accompanying harmonies. Within the same solo he would often return to it, transforming it each time. During Bill Evans's improvisations, an unheard, continuous self-editing was going on. He spared the listener his false starts and discarded ideas.*[4]

As with jazz soloists, so it is with organizational leaders. The competent ones hit the right notes, but the great ones are distinguished by how far ahead they are imagining and how they strategize possibilities, shape the contour of ideas, adapt and adjust in the midst of action, and resolve organizational tension. Both also face the same fundamental paradox: too much reliance on learned patterns (habitual or automatic thinking) tends to limit the risk taking necessary for creative growth, just as too much regulation and control restrict the interplay of ideas. In order for musicians and leaders in organizations to "strike a groove," they must suspend some degree of control and surrender to the flow.

Saxophonist Steve Lacy was talking about jazz when he described the inherent excitement *and* danger that come with improvisation, but he could just as easily have been describing the entrepreneurial rush that comes with venturing into new businesses and territories:

> *There is a freshness, a certain quality which can only be obtained by improvisation . . . It is something to do with the "edge," always being*

*on the brink of the unknown and being prepared for the leap. And when you go out there you have all your years of preparation and all your sensibilities and your prepared means but it is a leap into the unknown.*[5]

Being on the "brink of the unknown," on the "edge," and leaping in—this is an experience common to all those who take the risk to innovate. The experience is at once exhilarating and terrifying.

In a 2007 interview, the late Steve Jobs discussed the risk involved in innovation in words that would resonate with jazz musicians. Discussing his then-current challenge at Apple, he said: "There's a lot of things that are risky right now. If you could see to the other side and say 'yes this could be huge'—but there's a period of risk, no one's ever done it before." It's interesting that Jobs has articulated the same dilemma jazz improvisers face. You look out over what might happen and know that there's risk involved. But at some moment, you have to say yes, and Jobs adds his inimitable enthusiasm—"this could be huge." The interviewer then asked him if he had an example of a product that involves some kind of risk that might lead to huge benefits, but for which he has no guarantee. Jobs was careful not to disclose what he had in mind because he was experiencing that risky "yes" at that very moment. Instead, he replied that he had an example but "cannot say" right now.

In fact, we now know that Jobs was referring to the development of the iPad, but back then there was no guarantee the iPad would succeed—no way of knowing if it would be a "huge" commercial success or a flop as the Apple Newton had been. Jobs was doing what jazz musicians do all the time, living and acting in the unknown and loving every minute of it. As he told the interviewer, "when you feel like that, that's a great thing. That's what keeps you coming to work in the morning and it tells you there's something exciting around the next corner."[6]

In that same spirit, jazz historian Ted Gioia asks readers to imagine what it would be like for icons of other art forms to work under the same conditions that jazz musicians do:

> *Imagine T.S. Eliot giving nightly poetry readings at which, rather than reciting set pieces, he was expected to create impromptu poems—different ones each night, sometimes recited at a fast clip; imagine giving Hitchcock or Fellini a handheld motion picture camera and asking them to film something, anything—at that very moment, without the benefits of script, crew, editing, or scoring; imagine Matisse or Dali giving nightly exhibitions of their skills— exhibitions at which paying audiences would watch them fill up canvas after canvas with paint, often with only two or three minutes devoted to each "masterpiece."*[7]

Or imagine, for that matter, the CEO of a global petroleum giant having to react on the fly to a fatal explosion and burgeoning environmental disaster with virtually no useful script to follow, no sure solution to the blown-out wellhead, and no idea when or where the damage might stop. Tony Hayward might well have benefited from a few nights at the improv.

Weick has a favorite anecdote to drive home this idea of improvisation as an exhilarating (and sometimes terrifying) combination of exploration, constant experimentation, and tinkering with the unknown and often unknowable. A group of Hungarian soldiers were hiking in the Alps and got lost. After wandering aimlessly for days, some had given up hope of being found, while others had resigned themselves to dying. Until, that is, one of the soldiers found a map in his pocket. He used the map to help his fellow soldiers get their bearings and feel comfortable that they were headed in a hopeful direction. Indeed, the group finally did return safely. Only then did they realize that the map that saved their lives was of the Pyrenees Mountains, not the Alps.

To Weick, the story demonstrates that you should not fall in love with strategic plans, that when you are lost and face a radically unfamiliar situation, "any old map will do"—that is, any plan will work because it will turn you into a learner by helping you take action and venture forth into the unknown mindfully. You take a few steps and then new pathways emerge as you discover what to do next. Having a map helped turn the soldiers into learners precisely *because* they were able to experiment; with each tentative path, they compared their progress to the map, and this comparison heightened their awareness. They became more mindful. They could see more features of the landscape that might have gone unnoticed. The Pyrenees map tracked a different range, but it served to orient the soldiers and gave them a temporary sense of confidence that there was enough structure within the chaos and a loose belief that if they started down the path, they would eventually find their way out of their dilemma. Taking action turned them into learners. In short: Act first "as if" this will work; pay attention to what shows up; venture forth; make sense later.

The English Romantic age poet John Keats was getting at much the same idea when he praised Shakespeare for his "negative capability"—the ability "of being in uncertainties, Mysteries, doubts without any irritable reaching after fact & reason." Keats's fellow Romantic, Samuel Taylor Coleridge, wrote about what he called the "willing suspension of disbelief" that allows readers to fully enter into a fantastical tale. Both concepts partake of the fundamental nature of improvisation: sometimes leadership means letting go of the dream of certainty, leaping in, acting first, and reflecting later on the impact of the action.

I was once asked to play at a club in Cleveland with a jazz quartet that included members I had never before met, including a singer I had never accompanied. They called a hard bebop tune, and within a few measures, it was clear that the singer didn't really know the song very well and became disoriented. What to do? Players looked confused, and a few dropped out and looked around at each other. The drummer and the bass player kept going, but clearly they were about to stop. I was terrified and, for a few moments, frozen. So I just began to play a few notes, restating the melody in the original key. The sax player and bass player heard what I was up to and jumped in. The singer picked up the melody and started following it, making up new words. Within a few seconds, we were grooving again.

That's Keats's negative capability in action, but it's a good lesson for leaders, too, especially when the wheels are starting to come off and it's impossible to get enough information for a fully coherent plan. Do what jazz players do. Do what Shakespeare did. Act, and pay attention to what unfolds as you go.

For decades, the assumption has been that management is the art of planning, organizing, deciding, and controlling. But planning of necessity becomes unreliable when the environment grows unpredictable and unstable; organizing looks quite different viewed from the perspective of open-source innovation; deciding is not so much a rational, deductive conclusion as it is a product of ongoing relational exchanges; and controlling seems impossible in a world of networks. What we need to add to our list of managerial skills is improvisation— the art of adjusting, flexibly adapting, learning through trial-and-error initiatives, inventing ad hoc responses, and discovering as you go.

One popular story often associated with leadership holds that leaders master the skills and tools associated with strategy (such as financial and market analysis), much as people learn to play music by mastering scales, arpeggios, and other exercises. Business schools reinforce this model and sometimes treat learning as if knowledge were an object transferred between brains—what Paulo Freire called the "banking concept" of education. In this view, knowledge is a currency first deposited inside the head, then aggregated and detached in separate clusters that can be transferred, accumulated, and consumed.

In today's dynamic world, though, quickly unlearning old habits, routines, and strategies can often be as important as learning them in the first place. GE offers a case in point. Until the financial crisis that began in 2007, GE was convinced that its financial arm, GE Capital, was the goose that laid the golden eggs. Not only was GE Capital hugely profitable in itself, it required almost no new capital investment, such as factories, to sustain itself. Then came the crash, and the golden eggs turned rotten overnight. Suddenly, GE's credit rating was being downgraded from triple-A, and the company had to cut its dividend for the first time since the Great Depression, even with Warren Buffett riding to the rescue with a $3 billion investment.

Today, GE is stressing what it used to do so well in the past—making things, from light bulbs to jet engines, not just loans. But CEO and Chairman Jeffrey Immelt is also helping the company's next generation of leaders unlearn old ways by having them study and spend time with organizations as diverse as Google and the United States Military Academy at West Point—Google for its "constant entrepreneurship," as Immelt told the *New York Times*, and West Point for its "adaptability" and "resiliency" in highly dynamic and shifting circumstances.[8]

Sometimes it's in the context of breakdowns, even crises, that learning comes most alive. When there's a breakdown, managers have to do what jazz players yearn to do—abandon routines and respond in the moment. Faced with crisis, leaders often respond from their gut, sometimes discovering skills they never knew they had and solutions they had never previously imagined.

## On the Way to Yes—Abandoning Routines

In my high school and college years, I had a number of jazz idols, beginning with the pianist Oscar Peterson. Peterson could swing hard and play complex harmonies and lightning-fast licks—plus, he had the technique of a world-class concert pianist. I would listen to his recordings for hours, marveling at how flawless his playing was. Later, when I began to play professionally, I was stunned to learn that among some jazz musicians Peterson is not so highly regarded. As one of my friends said, "he can swing, but he's simply too perfect." What he meant, I came to understand, was that while Peterson had mastered the clean and perfect phrases that were his signature, often at breathtaking speed, his licks varied little if at all from number to number.

In effect, Peterson was saying the same "yes to the mess" just about every time he sat down at the piano, relying on catch phrases that became clichés until the playing itself grew programmatic. The pure sounds were there, the pyrotechnics he was famous for, but not the struggle that goes with improvisation, the willingness to stretch into the unfamiliar. As the composer-pianist Keith Jarrett once put it, in words that apply equally to jazz and business, "the music is struggle. You have to want to struggle. And what most leaders are the victim of is the freedom not to struggle. And then that's the end of it. Forget it!"[9]

If jazz has an exact anti-Peterson, it might be saxophonist Sonny Rollins. Many consider Rollins the greatest living improviser. He takes risks and tries new styles, forever stretching himself beyond his own familiar limitations. Among musicians, Rollins is almost as famous for his mistakes as he is for his "successful" innovations—wild experiments that have crashed grandly in ways that would embarrass most players. Fellow sax player Ronnie Scott contrasted Peterson's flawless prerehearsed solos with the risk taking of Rollins, who attempts to transform the harmonic and melodic materials that the tune presents:

> *Oscar Peterson is a very polished, technically immaculate performer, who—I hope he wouldn't mind me saying so—trots out these fantastic things that he has perfected, and it really is a remarkable performance. Whereas Sonny Rollins, he could go on one night and maybe it's disappointing, and another night he'll just take your breath away by his*

*kind of imagination and so forth. And it would be different every night with Rollins.*[10]

Rollins's deep commitment to staying open and responsive has led him down some unusual byways. Throughout the 1950s, he was a well-known and successful jazz musician, playing and recording with such greats as Miles Davis, Thelonious Monk, John Coltrane, Clifford Brown, Max Roach, and Art Blakey. But in 1959, Rollins mysteriously quit playing. Rumors circulated that he was sick or maybe suffering from drug addiction, but in fact he had quit because he had gotten tired of hearing himself playing the same phrases and licks in solo after solo.

Rollins wanted to break himself of the habit of playing what he had been hearing himself play, so for three years he went to the Williamsburg Bridge near his home in the Lower East Side of Manhattan, found a place under the surface of the bridge where he could be alone, and played his saxophone. Each time he heard a phrase that sounded like one of his familiar routines, he stopped, waited a moment, then played something he hadn't heard before. At the end of three years, he recorded an album with Jim Hall on guitar, Bob Cranshaw on bass, and Ben Riley on drums, and dedicated the album to the location he had found to reinvent himself. The title of the album is, simply, *The Bridge*.

At first, *The Bridge* was not well received by critics, partially because the music was such a dramatic departure from Rollins's previous style. Now it's considered a classic recording—on most critics' list of the ten most important jazz recordings ever made. In fact, here's how Rollins talks about how he approaches his art:

*As soon as I hear myself playing a familiar melody I take the mouthpiece out of my mouth. I let some measures go by. Improvising means coming in with a completely clean slate from the first note . . . the most important thing is to get away from fixed functions.*[11]

Rollins's efforts to unlearn his successful routines was an affirmative move. He was letting go of the familiar and comfortable in order to welcome new possibilities and opportunities. A quarter-century later, Intel's Andy Grove did almost exactly the same thing.

Grove is popularly credited with ingeniously, strategically, and deliberately leading Intel into the microprocessor industry, but as Grove himself recounted in his memoir, the real story is quite different.[12] The success of Intel was largely a matter of the top leadership team saying yes to the mess.

Intel is known today for its microprocessors, but for much of its early life, the company's success was built on DRAM technology (for dynamic random access memory), and by the mid-1980s, Japanese DRAM competition was severely eroding Intel's profit, from $198 million in 1984 to less than $2 million in 1985. Looking backward, the moral would seem to have been obvious: find another field to conquer. But Intel, in Kierkegaard's phrase, was "living forward," and Intel's scientists, technologists, sales force, and even its customers were so familiar with the existing processes that they could not imagine Intel *not* focusing on DRAM.

Nor was a fresh solution readily presenting itself. Intel's initial progress in microprocessors was somewhere between accidental and clandestine. An Intel manager invented the microprocessor inadvertently while developing technology for a calculator, but Intel strategists barely noticed the market potential of the discovery, even though microprocessors were proving to be very profitable. So powerful was the comfort of the company's past experiences that it continued to overwhelm external reality until, finally, Grove had his own "unlearning" moment.

As Grove tells the story in *Only the Paranoid Survive*, "I looked out the window at the Ferris wheel of the Great America amusement park revolving in the distance when I turned back to [Intel cofounder] Gordon [Moore], and I asked, 'If we got kicked out and the Board brought in a new CEO, what do you think he would do?'

Gordon answered without hesitation, 'He would get us out of memories.' I stared at him, numb, then said, 'Why shouldn't you and I walk out the door, come back, and do it ourselves?'"[13] And thus was born Grove's famous first step in attacking difficult problems: "Set aside everything you know."

"Welcome to the new Intel," Grove announced in a speech not long afterward. Intel went from being a company that makes memory chips to a company that focused on microprocessors, a move that quickly became hugely profitable. But to get there, he and Moore had to let go of the routines that were the secret to past success. Only by unlearning old routines were they able to open themselves to new opportunities and see the potential coming from an unexpected direction. To develop the dynamic capability that would carry the company forward, they had to step outside of themselves, something else jazz players are constantly called to do.

## "Take a Knee"

On April 3, 2003, during the early weeks of the Iraq War, Lt. Col. Chris Hughes led the U.S. 101st Battalion into volatile Najaf, on a crucial and sensitive mission to meet with Grand Ayatollah Ali al-Sistani, who was in residence at the mosque—the third holiest site for Shiite Muslims because it is the Imam Ali Mosque. That alone made the mission sensitive, but the Shiite high cleric was also crucial to establishing good relationships with the Iraqis. He had urged Muslims to remain calm and cooperate with U.S. forces, and now he was asking the U.S. Army for protection, the immediate reason for the 101st's mission.

Unfortunately, as the battalion neared the mosque, a rumor began to spread that the Americans intended to arrest the cleric and destroy the holy site. With that, Iraqi villagers suddenly turned on the U.S. troops. Indeed, within a split second, the situation changed dramatically. Now Hughes and the men under his command faced an angry standoff in highly uncertain territory. The soldiers were tense as an increasingly hostile crowd began to crowd in on them. "It seemed to turn like that, but it was a very deliberate turn," Hughes said later. "If somebody shot a round in the air, there was going to be some sort of massacre."

"Everybody smile!" he ordered his troops, as an embedded CBS News camera caught the scene. "Don't point your weapons at them. Take a knee! Relax!" The "take a knee" order seemed to buy time, so Hughes followed up by ordering his men to withdraw, and just as suddenly, the situation pivoted once more, and goodwill was restored.

Reporter Dan Baum later interviewed Hughes for a *New Yorker* account of the incident.[14] Where had he learned this strategy? Baum asked. How did he know that pointing his own rifle down and ordering his men to take a knee would tame the crowd? Nowhere, Hughes said in essence. He was making it up on the spot, as he went along.

At first glance, Hughes's answer would seem to align with the popular understanding of jazz musicians as free-spirited, free-form performers. But in reality his answer goes to the deeper nature of the art form. U.S. military training manuals generally teach two standard responses to situations such as Hughes and the 101st Battalion faced: use helicopter blades to push away angry crowds or fire warning shots. The last step in the training is the final solution: shoot to kill. So when Hughes ordered his men to "get down on one knee and smile," he was in fact improvising. But his solution was also the result of relentless learning and a disciplined imagination that, in an instant, took into account the complex tribal dynamics that all foreign troops faced in Iraq. Hughes threw out the rules, to be sure, but he didn't throw out his deeper engagement and his deeper desire to express respect toward the Iraqis. Even under the intense pressure of the moment, he managed to stay fully engaged in the details *and* in the aggregate. That's what made the difference, and that's great jazz in a nutshell.

This book challenges the myths or belief systems we hold about leadership. It's often assumed that without singular direction, groups turn chaotic or unruly. What we are learning, though, is that without being guided by an outside entity or prescripted plan, a system can self-organize and produce even more efficient and effective outcomes. Think how different this model is from the one we have been taught. We were told that social systems need hierarchy to function and coordinate. But when birds flock, when cities form and expand, there is no controlling singular force. *Individuals act unpredictably, and yet a coherent and productive organization emerges. Just as in jazz.* The message is provocative: an emergent system is smarter than the individual members. And systems grow smarter over time. The jazz mind-set is one that recognizes the emerging coherence amid constant flux.

In a system of distributed, decentralized control, what are the implications for leadership? How does someone lead "structured chaos"? What is the role of the leader in a group creation? Leaders often must act without full awareness of the consequences of their action, even without any full articulation of what the plan might be or how it is likely to change in progress. That's organizational life in the twenty-first century. Frequently, only after action is initiated are actual goals and preferences discovered, and it's only in hindsight that we understand what motivated our judgments and actions. Jazz is all about repeating a theme. In this book, I am laying out the principles of jazz performance to help executives, managers, and leaders, in whatever context, elevate performance by showing them how to break the mold and move beyond the expected.

# CHAPTER TWO

# "Yes to the Mess"

## Developing Affirmative Competence

We all know about messes. Messes are big problems. They gum up the works, retard progress, and deface our records—corporate and personal—with ugly black marks. Little wonder that a manager's first impulse is to guard vigilantly against messes: to eliminate them if possible and clean them up expeditiously when they happen, including often getting rid of those responsible. This habit of housecleaning is hard to break, but consider the example of Amazon.com. In 2006, Amazon launched Unbox, a video download service that within a week was pronounced "a complete and utter failure." Unbox took as long as seven hours to download a ninety-minute movie, and once downloaded, the movie could not be shown on any other device. And as if that weren't bad enough, the Amazon player would intermittently launch itself!

This was undoubtedly a mess with many faces, and one might well imagine that the design team behind Unbox was in big trouble. But Amazon CEO Jeff Bezos took a different approach. "The thing that

allows for all the teams to come together after a failure is the recognition that this is just a first failure [for the project]," Bezos later
reflected. "If we have conviction, that gives us energy to pursue
[another] approach."[1]

The Amazon founder and CEO was doing what jazz musicians
have been doing since the art form began: saying yes to the mess,
learning while doing, rejecting habitual behavior and a predictable
outcome in favor of experimentation and progress. This story isn't
about linear growth or tangential growth through acquisition. It's
about taking action, revising assumptions, valuing learning from failures, trying again, and discovering as you go, with an underlying confidence in the competence of the group.

When Bezos called Unbox "just a first failure," he was advocating essentially an improvisational mind-set. He echoed the jazz ethos
again when he said of the failed launch, *"If you only extend into places
where your skill sets serve you, your skills become outmoded."* Jazz musicians and organizational leaders both need to be constantly challenging routines and attempting new approaches. Only by taking risks
can they expand action repertoires, replenish knowledge, and renew
old skills.

Herman Miller—the Michigan-based manufacturer of high-end
office furniture such as the Equa and Aeron chairs, as well as the
inventor of the office cubicle—consistently rates as one of *Fortune*
magazine's "most admired companies," and with good cause. Beginning in the early 1990s, the company committed itself to promoting
sustainability. Since then, it has tracked every chemical used in each of
its products as a way to eliminate harmful substances from the entire
production chain. Renewable energy and recycled and recyclable
materials are also high on Herman Miller's list. Consistent with these
efforts, the company in 1993 hired architect William McDonough to
design a "green" manufacturing plant.

McDonough's design makes efficient use of resources such as energy
and water, as well as reducing waste and pollution to lessen the impact

on the environment. As a kind of crown to his efforts, McDonough topped the Holland, Michigan, building with an innovative "green" roof of soil, vegetables, and flowers. The benefits of the living roof are many: it decreases temperatures in the summer and retains heat in the winter, reduces storm-water runoff, filters carbon dioxide out of the air, and insulates the building for sound. But McDonough's cutting-edge lid also had one unintended consequence.

Shortly after the building was finished, large colonies of aggressive wasps began to dwell in the vegetation. This left company executives with a dilemma—how to get rid of these pesky and potentially dangerous wasps. The conventional method is to use pesticides, but this flew in the face of the green ideology. So someone came up with a brilliant idea: Herman Miller imported 600,000 bees in twelve hives and established them around the rooftop grounds. Eventually, the wasps were persuaded to leave. The bees began to cross-pollinate the surrounding fields, spreading wildflowers and filling their hives with honey, which led to a second but much sweeter dilemma—what to do with all of this new product. Then someone had another brilliant idea: bottle it. Now, visitors to the plant receive a gift just for showing up—a four-ounce bottle of Herman Miller honey, straight from the rooftop.

The philosopher Søren Kierkegaard wrote that life is understood backward, but lived forward. Herman Miller's experience with its green building provides a good example. In hindsight, it's easy to see how the company fashioned a solution that further enhanced its reputation as a forward-thinking enterprise with a well-developed social conscience. Living forward, though, the story is far more convoluted.

Executives certainly must have anticipated some unseen challenges with such a unique building design, but when they realized they had created a home for aggressive wasps, my guess is that more than a few of them were surprised, even irritated, and ready to reach for the nearest textbook solution—a heavy dose of pesticides, even though that would have defeated the original purpose of creating a green factory.

Instead, the company went, in a sense, even deeper into the mess, importing twelve hives of 600,000 honeybees to neutralize the wasps. Failure at this stage could have left the company with a huge problem to clean up—even angrier wasps and potentially half a million bees swarming all over the place—and failure was always a possibility. Honeybees are generally effective against wasps, but this was an untested rooftop micro-environment where anything might happen. But the experiment did work, and the company salvaged an added positive by creating bottles of honey that it could then give away as a goodwill gesture—and a reminder of its commitment to sustainability—to thousands of visitors. This is not only saying yes to the mess; this is an unrelenting, affirmative mind-set, exactly what jazz musicians most need.

Jazz players assume that no matter how incoherent or unpredictable the current situation appears, they'll find some positive pathway out, some creative possibility to uncover and explore. Without such a mind-set (a bias toward positivity), they would have trouble performing at all because, by the very nature of the art form, they find themselves in the middle of messes all the time. Jazz musicians can't stop in the middle of a number to problem solve or put situations in order or say to other players, "I don't like those notes you played. They didn't match with what I had in mind, so let's go back and do it over." The major reason why improvisation works is that the musicians say an implicit yes to each other. Like the managers at Herman Miller who found ways to get rid of wasps *and* make honey, jazz musicians succeed because they have faith that whatever is happening has potential to lead in innovative directions.

Because jazz improvisation borders on chaos and incoherence, it begs the question of how order emerges. Unlike other art forms and other forms of organized activity that attempt to rely on a predeveloped plan, improvisation is widely open to transformation, redirection, and unprecedented turns. Since we cannot rely on blueprints and can never know for certain where the music is going, we can only make guesses and anticipate possible paths based on what has already happened. As jazz critic Ted Gioia writes: "The improviser may be unable to look ahead at what he is going to play, but he can look behind at what he has just played; thus each new musical phrase can be shaped with relation to what has gone before. He creates his form *retrospectively* [italics added]."[2]

A jazz musician might begin by playing a virtual random series of notes, with little or no intention as to how it will unfold. These notes become the materials to shape and work out, like pieces of a puzzle. The improviser then begins to enter into a dialogue with the material: prior selections begin to fashion subsequent ones as themes are aligned and reframed in relation to prior patterns.

In a sense, jazz improvisation is much like *bricolage*, the art of using whatever is at hand. The anthropologist Claude Lévi-Strauss first coined the term bricolage; those who practice it are *bricoleurs*. They tinker with a myriad of disparate materials and put seemingly unrelated things together into some semblance of order. They are junk collectors who bring order out of chaos. Both bricoleurs and jazz musicians examine and query the raw materials available and then entice order, creating unique combinations as they work through their resources.

I'm reminded of the story of a man in upstate New York who had accumulated several pieces of junk in his front yard. To his neighbors, and to anyone who happened to see the mess, it looked like a myriad collection of scrap iron and diverse parts he had accumulated—mismatched gears, springs, old tires. Yet he was able to "see" order in the junk. From this pile, he could see order and built a tractor out of it. That's bricolage. Just as that bricoleur assumed there must be a tractor somewhere in that pile of junk, so the jazz improviser assumes that there is a melody to be worked out from the morass of rhythms and chord changes. As new phrases or chord changes are introduced, the improviser makes connections between old and new material. In the absence of a rational plan, retrospective sense making lends a seemingly purposeful and coherent inevitability to what is, in truth, spontaneous action.[3]

Comedy improvisers have a deliberate phrase to capture this: "yes and . . ." When two improvisers are working together (think of the old Drew Carey show *Whose Line Is It Anyway?*), they make continuous offers back and forth. The other actor's responsibility is to accept the offer and move it forward.[4] Similarly, the jazz improviser attends closely to what is happening, seeing the potential for embellishing on motifs, linking familiar with new utterances, and adjusting to unanticipated musical cues that reframe previous material. In this continual exchange, each interpretation has implications for where to proceed. Jazz improvisation involves constant attention to such musical "yes and . . ." cues. There's always an obligation to look back on what has happened and extend it.

Organizations tend to forget how much improvisation, bricolage, and retrospective sense making managers need to complete daily tasks. In an effort to control outcomes and deskill tasks, managers often attempt to break complex jobs down into formal descriptions of work procedures that people can follow automatically. In a perfectly rational world, such strategy makes perfect sense, but that's rarely the way work actually gets done. Many, perhaps most, tasks in organizations are indeterminate, undertaken by people with limited foresight. To meet their duties, employees frequently need to apply their own resourcefulness, cleverness, and pragmatism. They play with various possibilities, recombining and reorganizing, to find solutions by relating the dilemma they face to the familiar context that preceded it.

Consider the study of Xerox's training for service technician representatives. In an effort to down-skill the task of machine repair, the trainers attempted to document every imaginable breakdown in copiers so that when technicians arrived to repair a machine, they simply looked it up in the manual and followed a predetermined decision tree to perform a series of tests that dictated a repair procedure. The premise was that they could devise a diagnostic sequence to respond to the machine's predictable problems. However, the study revealed that no amount of documentation could include enough contextual information to understand every problem.

Julian Orr relates the story of a technical rep confronting a machine with error codes and malfunctions that were not congruent with the diagnostic blueprint.[5] Nothing similar had been documented or covered in his training, and both the original rep and the technical specialist he called in to help were baffled. To simply give up the repair effort and replace the machine would have been a solution, but this would have meant loss of face with the customer—an unacceptable course of action. After exhausting the approaches suggested by the diagnostic, they attempted to make sense of this anomaly by connecting it to previous experiences and stories they had heard others relate. Finally, after a five-hour session of trials and errors, they came upon a solution.[6]

So it is with many jobs in organizations. They require bricolage— fumbling around, experimenting, and patching together an understanding of problems from bits and pieces of experience, improvising with the materials at hand. Few problems provide their own definitive solutions.

The date was January 11, 1980. I had just joined the Tommy Dorsey Band under the direction of Buddy Morrow, and two weeks into the job, I was still struggling. I couldn't read music and had been faking my way through several of the numbers. Morrow would have replaced me in a heartbeat, I think, but we were in the middle of a long tour and it's hard to pick up a piano player on the fly. On this particular Friday evening, we were playing a concert at the Omni in Houston, sharing the bill with Count Basie and his band. The marquee was full, and the venue was huge, with a crowd of at least five thousand expected. I don't know if I have ever been more nervous in my life.

In the middle of our set, the rhythm section—piano, bass, and drums—was to play a song that featured a young clarinetist named Ken Peplowski. He would go on to become a big recording star for Concord records. We had played together previously in Cleveland, so I was familiar with him, but the rhythm section was still finding its way, and that's where the trouble began. We had just come to the part of the song in which our section was supposed to drop out and allow Peplowski to play solo, but somehow the signals got crossed, and suddenly I was the one playing by myself. I remember looking up startled at Peplowski as he raised one eyebrow and said, "Take it. It's yours." All I could think at that moment was, "Oh my God!"

I didn't have many options. I was relatively familiar with the song but had never played it solo, so I put my head down and played a series of random notes. There were no drums and no bass player. Just me on the piano. Sweating and anxious, feeling that all ten thousand eyes out in the audience were bearing down on me, I repeated the random notes, this time adding chords from the left hand as I kept going with the beat and telling myself, "just keep playing and something good will come out of these notes." And soon I had used those notes to develop a theme—repeating, extending, modifying, and completely making it up as I went along. I said yes to the mess I was in and followed what I was hearing myself play.

For reasons I still cannot explain, I took two verses. I have a tape of that performance, and when I listen to it, I still laugh out loud. My playing was inspired and, frankly, risky, but beyond that, something very strange had happened. I played phrases I had never heard before.

Perhaps because there were no drums or bass to support the rhythm, my left hand started playing this swinging boogie-woogie bass. At the end of the first verse, I heard Peplowski say, "Yeah." I remember hearing someone in the crowd scream out the same thing, "Yeah!" As my solo ended and the band came back in, the audience applauded loudly.

That night was my turning point as a pianist. My sense of identity was transformed. Before, I had seen myself mostly as a fumbling, amateur player; now I knew I was capable of performing decent jazz solos, including licks that I had never practiced. Even now, although I am not a full-time musician and in fact rarely play, I still have this "shadow" identity that accompanies me. I'm a jazz musician.

I had a similar situation when I was teaching in a program for high-level executives a few years ago. One of my colleagues had a crisis and had to miss class. I was, she assured me, the *only* one who could teach it on such short notice. (Some friend!)

I was vaguely familiar with the case study that was to be the subject of that day's class, but the full details of the case were escaping me, and as I made my way to the venue, I realized how anxious I was. I didn't have that much lecture material. I was clearly not adequately prepared. I began to imagine that I was going to embarrass myself. I fretted over standing up in front of the class with nothing to say. I even imagined ways I could get out of it. Could I call in sick? Or start by announcing that this module would last only one hour, just long enough for me to trot out a few well-worn clichés and get out of there? An hour I could handle; two hours seemed like an eternity. Then I started to dwell upon the "students" who would inevitably be disappointed— these demanding, self-absorbed executives.

I arrived at the classroom, looked out at the executives in the room, and suddenly realized that I was so absorbed with my own fears that I had forgotten about them. I had unwittingly been thinking of the students as a monolithic group of impatient, moody, bottom-line suits, demanding that I keep them entertained. I had to start somehow, so I blurted out the first words that came to me: "I'm really excited to be here." The words came out slowly and self-consciously. Maybe they won't notice that I'm telling a half-truth. I feared I sounded awkward, as if I was trying to squeeze a tennis ball through a garden hose. And of course, I meant "excited" in a very particular, nervous sense. What surprised me, though, and what I remember so clearly even now is that when I said, "I'm really excited to be here," something changed. The students started to look slightly different. Suddenly, a few of them actually looked friendly.

Next, as if I were playing jazz, I tried a slight variation of my previous phrasing: "I'm pleased we could be here," basically repeating my previous sentence. Now what? "What a treat it is to be able to spend time with so many experienced leaders who have so much wisdom." I noticed a few of them smiling, so I took a deep breath and continued, and in a sudden, unspoken flash, the midcareer execs changed before my very eyes. These were good people, eager to learn, with a wealth of wisdom, and much to my surprise, I was actually starting to feel some excitement.

"I'm interested in innovation," I continued, "and I realize that you've all had lots of experience with the dynamics of innovation and leadership in your organizations, and I'm looking forward to learning from each other." And then suddenly it all became true, and the next two hours flew by as these twenty-five executives and I had this fascinating conversation about innovation and leadership.

Why? What had happened? It's not that I changed my belief and then changed what I said. Rather, I changed my words first. I started to act as if this were true and then eventually started to believe it, and these hopeful words changed the world right in front of me.

To be sure, I could have gone back to the old rules and routines as a way to relieve my anxiety. I could have brought in a series of Power-Point slides, a presentation I could do in my sleep that would impress enough of them to get me through the day. (And, of course, I had done that in the past, too.) I could have explained that the scheduled instructor couldn't make it, that I'm a last-minute substitute, lowering their expectations so that they would forgive whatever I did as inexperience and my being a good citizen for coming in at the last minute. Alternatively, I could have delivered a lecture on some other topic I'm very familiar with, à la Oscar Peterson trotting out clichés. That would have worked. I had done things like this in the past, too. Or I could have stayed aloof from the students, avoiding embarrassing mistakes by saying things that are safe or unassailable. Instead, I said yes to the mess, stayed actively engaged with the interaction, and had one of the most interesting two hours of my teaching career. We started as a class; we ended as a community.

## Jazz as Continual Negotiation: Saying Yes to the Groove

Although jazz players are best known for their soloing, jazz itself in the final analysis is an ongoing social accomplishment. Players are in a continual dialogue and exchange with one another. Improvisers enter a flow of ongoing invention, a combination of accents, cymbal crashes, and changing harmonic patterns that interweave throughout the structure of the song. They are engaged with continual streams of activity: interpreting others' playing and anticipating based on harmonic patterns and rhythmic conventions, while simultaneously attempting to shape their own creations and relate them to what they have heard.

Jazz improvisation is an emergent, elusive, vital process. At any moment, a player can take the music in a new direction, defying expectations and triggering others to reinterpret what they have just heard. Trumpeter Wynton Marsalis compares improvisation to working out ideas in democratic groups, in terms strikingly reminiscent of John Dewey's dictum that genuine learning is by nature a participative, democratic experience.

*Groups of people can get together and the process of their negotiation*
*can have an integrity, and the fact that they can get together and have*
*a dialogue and work—it's like what the UN does. They sit down, and*
*they try to work things out. It's like any governing body. It's like a*
*wagon train, you know.*[7]

Pianist Tommy Flanagan discussed his duo albums with Hank Jones
and Kenny Barron in equally communitarian terms:

*You don't know what the other player is going to play, but on listen-*
*ing to the playback, you hear that you related your part very quickly*
*to what the other player played just before you. It's like a message that*
*you relay back and forth . . . You want to achieve that kind of commu-*
*nication when you play. When you do, your playing seems to be mak-*
*ing sense. It's like a conversation.*[8]

In order for jazz to work, players must develop a remarkable degree
of empathic competence, a mutual orientation to one another's
unfolding. They continually take one another's musical ideas into context as constraints and facilitations in guiding their musical choices.
Here's what saxophonist Lee Konitz has to say about this interactive
interplay and the challenges it constantly presents:

*I want to relate to the bass player and the piano player and the drum-*
*mer, so that I know at any given moment what they are all doing. The*
*goal is always to relate as fully as possible to every sound that everyone*
*is making . . . but whew! It's very difficult for me to achieve. At differ-*
*ent points, I will listen to any particular member of the group and relate*
*to them as directly as possible in my solo.*[9]

Players are continuously shaping their statements in anticipation of
others' expectations, approximating and predicting what others might
say based on what has already happened.

Traditional models of organization and group design feature static principles in which fluctuations and change are seen as disruptions to be controlled and avoided. Jazz bands are flexible, self-designed systems that seek a state of dynamic synchronization, a balance between order and disorder: a "built-in instability." In jazz, ongoing negotiation becomes very important when something interrupts interactive coherence. Given the possibility of disorientation and miscalculations, players must be able to rely on one another to adjust, to amend direction. Drummer Max Roach recalls a performance of "Night in Tunisia" when Dizzy Gillespie and his fellow players lost the sense of a common beat.

> *When the beat got turned around, it went for about 8 bars. In such a case, someone has to lay out. You can't fight it. Dizzy stopped first because he heard what was happening quicker than the rest of us, and he didn't know where "one" was. Then it was up to Ray Brown and Bishop and myself. One of us had to stop, so Bishop waved off. Then it was up to Ray Brown and myself to clear it up. Almost immediately, we found the common "one" and the others came back in without the public realizing what had happened.[10]*

When the players do successfully achieve a mutual orientation to the beat, they develop what they call a "pocket," or what some refer to as "achieving a groove." Establishing a groove is the goal of every jazz performance. Groove refers to the dynamic interplay within an established beat. It occurs when the rhythm section "locks in" together, when members have a common sense of the beat and meter. Establishing a groove, however, is more than simply playing the correct notes. It involves a shared "feel" for the rhythmic thrust. Once a group shares this common rhythm, it begins to assume a momentum, as if having a life of its own separate from the individual members.

When musicians "hit the groove," they don't experience themselves as the source of that activity. This is ironic in a time when we put so much emphasis on autonomous skilled agents making rational, individual choices. When groups hit a groove they talk about it as if the source of this activity comes from somewhere else. They apply masterly skillful activity and yet remain radically open to the surrounding situation that is calling forth a response. Musicians often speak of such moments in sacred metaphors: the beauty, the ecstasy, the divine, the transcendent joy, the spiritual dimension associated with being carried by a force larger than themselves. They talk about these moments in language strikingly close to what has been described as an autotelic experience, or flow: a state of transcendence in which they are so absorbed in pursuit of the desired activity that they feel as if they are being carried away by a current, like being in a flow.

Not surprisingly, when musicians are able to successfully connect with one another at this level and establish a groove, they often find themselves able to perform beyond their capacity. This dimension is perhaps the most elusive, if vital characteristic of jazz improvisation. Pianist Fred Hersch recalls that playing with bassist Buster Williams inspired him to play differently:

> Buster made me play complex chords like Herbie Hancock sometimes plays—that I couldn't even sit down and figure out now. It's the effect of the moment and the effect of playing with Buster and really hearing everything, hearing all those figures.[11]

And Buster Williams recalls that when playing with Miles Davis, the music took on a life of its own.

> With Miles, it would get to the point where we followed the music rather than the music following us. We just followed the music wherever it wanted to go. We would start with a tune, but the way we played it, the music just naturally evolved.[12]

Imagine a self-organized flock of birds, wheeling this way and that. There's no single controller, and yet a discernible pattern emerges into the communal effect as a sort of natural art. That's really what jazz is at its best, something for all organizations to emulate. Wouldn't it be wonderful if leaders could create organizational cultures in which people are able to engage in skillful activity in the context of responsive others?

## Leading by Saying Yes to the Best of What Exists

The best leaders are not detached and predominantly analytic, although these are important skills to develop. The very best leaders know when it's important to be fully and passionately engaged in problems and situations, and for enhancing creativity and innovation, the crucial first step is an affirmative move.

Consider the story of Michelangelo and how he created his famous *David*. When Michelangelo was commissioned in 1501 to create a statue for a Florence cathedral, he carved it from a piece of marble that a previous sculptor, Agostino di Duccio, had worked with but discarded forty years earlier. Di Duccio presumably had been too frustrated to go on, and little wonder. Carving a complex figure from a resistant material demands strong problem-solving skills.

Author William Wallace describes the challenge Michelangelo faced:

> *Marble carving is hard work, loud and dirty. Every blow of hammer to chisel is a collision of metal against metal striking stone. Marble chips fly in all directions; the dust lies thick. Modern stone workers wear goggles; Michelangelo did not. He had to see the stone, to see each mark, to make tiny adjustments to the angle of his chisel and to the force of his blow. He could not afford to slip. One wrong stroke could break a finger, an arm, or worse. A figure comes alive only after thousands and thousands—tens of thousands—of perfectly directed hard and soft blows. Marble carving is difficult and unforgiving.*[13]

Given such challenges, how did Michelangelo succeed? Not by focusing on the problems as perhaps di Duccio did. Rather, Michelangelo looked at the discarded marble and saw his David already there in his full pose. What was needed, he said, was simply to "clear the rest of the marble away in order to bring David out." Michelangelo's primary concern wasn't the piece of rock itself and all the pitfalls of working with it. His first concern, his most vital energy, was devoted to forming an image of the perfect David before he ever put chisel to stone.

Critics and observers are still in awe of the result. Michelangelo's *David* was carved, according to historian Paul Johnson, "with almost atrocious skill and energy."[14] But the process and ultimate success began with mind-set—Michelangelo's ability to see David waiting to be realized from within that discarded chunk of marble. His *capacity* to imagine David in his pristine wholeness, to form a perfect image—this is an approach to learning that leads to bold innovation. (Later, by the way, the statue was seen as such a radical artistic achievement that it came to symbolize the identity of the entire community of Florence. Rather than placing it in the cathedral as originally commissioned, *David* was put on more public display in front of the town hall, the Palazzo Vecchio.)

Why is it often so hard to say yes to the unknown? Social psychologists and behavioral economists have shown that humans are profoundly loss averse: most people prefer avoiding a loss to acquiring a gain, especially in stressful times. Stress locks us into tunnel vision and leads us to adopt a siege mentality. We circle the wagons to avoid risk as best we can, but such a mind-set, while understandable, is self-limiting. Rather than saying yes to the mess, people cut short the discovery process, stop learning, and fail to notice opportunities.

Consider this example. As the stock market losses piled up through 2008 and into 2009, one very prestigious university saw a large portion of its endowment disappear. University leaders responded understandably by limiting spending, including hiring new faculty. Indeed, in some areas, the university stopped hiring altogether. But a less prestigious university, faced with the same proportional loss of its endowment, immediately saw this same situation as an opportunity. Administrators there realized that if one of the nation's top universities was no longer hiring, then more highly qualified and attractive candidates would be available—candidates who in previous years had been lost to schools with more glowing reputations. Yes, times were hard and not likely to improve soon, but the leaders of this university saw through the mess and found an unprecedented chance to take a giant leap forward.

This is the kind of move that is typical of a jazz mind-set and one of the core themes of this book. Jazz improvisers focus on discovery in times of stress. They know how to ensure that they don't get stuck in old habits even when reliable routines might seem like the quickest way to relieve anxiety. They interpret challenging situations so that fear does not limit choices and support the birth of good ideas. While there are no guarantees of outcomes, they realize the benefit of a mind-set that maximizes opportunities, understands the importance of intelligent risk taking, and most important, learns by saying yes and leaping in.

## Affirmative Competence

Researchers in a number of different fields have affirmed the transforming power of positive expectation. Patients often show marked biological and emotional improvements simply because they believe they are receiving helpful treatment, even though they have been given only sugar pills. The placebo effect has been widely documented, but this powerful anticipatory effect is not limited to our own expectations. The mere fact that others have positive expectations for our performance can shape outcome.[15]

Classroom research on self-fulfilling prophecy and the so-called Pygmalion effect has shown that when teachers are led to believe that one group of students is more intelligent and capable than other groups, the positive-expectation group will outperform their peers even though in actuality the students have been randomly distributed. So it is in the workplace as well. The anticipation of a good performance, the expectation of competency, sets up a self-reinforcing loop between the manager and employee as they co-shape one another's behavior. The manager's expectations hasten the results they predict because the manager has been cued to notice competence while attributing poor performance to some exogenous factor, which in turn triggers the worker to perform at a high level, reaffirming the manager's high expectations. High-performance groups tap into the power of expectation loops. They find subtle ways to invoke positive anticipation by focusing on success.

Sports psychologists are great proponents of expectation loops. In addition to superb physical attributes, many top professional athletes have learned to hone this affirmative competence, projecting detailed, positive guiding images as if they were already true. Studies of bowlers, for instance, have demonstrated that those who are most successful at deliberately focusing on successful outcomes perform at much higher levels than other competitors. The studies further suggest a strong difference between dwelling on eliminating obstacles and conjuring an image of success. Creating a self-script that says "avoid rolling a gutter ball"—an avoidance goal—can lend the gutter ball an ironically alluring quality. Successful self-monitoring athletes focus, instead, on a script of "finding the pocket and hitting the perfect strike."[16] Research suggests that positive self-monitoring is more likely to lead to effective performance than avoidance goals.[17]

By the late 1980s, Vietnam was in the midst of an ongoing tragedy: 60 percent to 70 percent of the children under the age of five were suffering from malnutrition. Multiple approaches had failed to lift the numbers. Dr. Jerry Sternin, working with Save the Children, had a unique idea. He saw that the traditional methods of intervention were not working, so one day he asked a woman in a village where he was working if there were any families whose children were *not* dying of malnutrition. In fact, there were. The villagers named one family in particular. Then Sternin did something unusual: he created a learning community among the villagers by helping them become inquirers, by creating a situation of discovery. He brought the families in the village together to study this successful family and helped them to ask questions. In the process, the families with weak and dying children learned things about a neighbor they had been living next to for years.[18]

It turns out that this family had been collecting shrimps and crabs from the rice field, adding them with greens and sweet potatoes to the kids' meals. This was contrary to the popular belief in the village that those foods should not be given to children, but in fact, this family was providing its children with a valuable source of protein. Having found "positive deviants" in the village—those who perform better than their peers with the same resources—Sternin then took a second, equally novel approach to distributing the learning. He arranged dialogues between the families—sessions in which they would cook, eat, and talk together. By the end of the year, a thousand children had been through these nutrition lessons, and 90 percent had recovered from malnutrition.

This is what improvisational leaders do. They come at challenges from different angles, ask more searching questions, and are born communitarians. They're not going for easy answers or living off of old routines and stale phrases. Instead of focusing on obstacles (a form of negative self-monitoring), they create openings by asking questions that entertain possibilities. They're looking for the groove, the flow, knowing that like Sternin, it might carry them somewhere they never expected to go, somewhere they never imagined they could get to. Critically, too, improvisational leaders assume that the improv will work: that the mess is only a way station on the path to a worthwhile destination. The message here is powerful: start by asking positive questions; foster dialogues, not monologues; and you can change the whole situation, maybe even your life.

## CHAPTER THREE

# Performing and Experimenting Simultaneously

## Embracing Errors as a Source of Learning

When Alan Mulally took over as CEO of Ford Motor Company in 2006, he inherited a company that had lost billions of dollars. To measure progress, Mulally asked his vice presidents and functional heads to come to meetings with color-coded reports: green for good, yellow for caution, red for problem areas. At the first few meetings, the managers showed up with their operations all coded green, until finally Mulally said, "You guys, you know we lost a few billion dollars last year. Is there anything that's *not* going well?" With that, one of the vice presidents, Mark Fields, spoke up. The Ford Edge, he reported, was experiencing technical problems and would not be ready for production and distribution as scheduled. There was silence in the room until

Mulally clapped and congratulated Fields. "Mark," he said, "I really appreciate your clear visibility."

Fields's disclosure and Mulally's response not only laid bare the difficulties with a key component of Ford's future, but also taught others in the room that it was OK to share errors. In the past, the vice presidents had been required to defend problems and disappointments, so they tended to avoid reporting them. Now, they knew they weren't going to be punished for making mistakes, and the effect was dramatic. "The next week the entire set of charts were all rainbows," Fields said later. Mulally agreed: "They don't bring their big books anymore because I'm not going to grind them with as many questions as I can to humiliate them."[1]

What does it mean to live in a team culture in which it is OK to bring your errors forward, to publicly discuss mistakes? The record is very clear: groups that have adapted these practices and leaders who promote them accelerate learning. *Failure, after all, is an inevitable part of risk and experimentation.* Indeed, it's often the pathway to discovery, especially in highly experimental and innovative cultures. But the value of tolerating errors extends as well to the day-to-day operations of complex systems and even to routine processes. In both instances, the fear of reporting mistakes can lead to failure and, sometimes, tragedy.

I ended the last chapter by suggesting that leaders begin by asking positive questions. I begin this chapter with the story of a leader asking, "Is there anything that's not going well?" This seems like a contradiction. However, upon closer inspection, these two moves are related. They are both affirmative moves and questions that validate experimentation and learning. When Mulally asked people to share their mistakes, he too was saying yes in a very profound way. He was saying, "Yes, I expect us to experiment and not everything will work out the way we had hoped. And yes, it is safe to talk about disappointments and bring them forth so that we can all learn as we go. Don't hide from mistakes. Use them as an occasion for learning and improvement."

## Imperfection and Forgiveness

Miles Davis, the great trumpeter, bandleader, and composer, had a favorite saying about jazz musicians: "If you're not making a mistake, it's a mistake." There's lots of wisdom in that. Davis was talking about the importance of continuing to take risks, to gamble, and to try new possibilities, because when you do, something new is likely to happen; some fresh discovery is waiting just around the next musical corner.

The fact is, errors, mistakes, fluffs, boots, whatever you want to call them, are endemic to jazz. When players aim beyond their reach, when they perform without a safety net or any clear plan or guarantee of outcome, mistakes are bound to happen. Often, there are discrepancies between intention and action: Sometimes the hands fail to play what the inner ear imagines. Other times, musicians misinterpret cues or simply play the wrong notes. They're human, after all, but what they don't do if they want to prosper in the art form is censure each other for the mistakes they make. Instead, jazz players learn to approach errors as if they are simply another suggestion for ways to proceed. They might repeat the mistake, amplify it, and develop it further until it becomes a new pattern. In essence, the players are constantly saying to each other, "Yes, let's see where this leads." Appreciating the affirmative potential in every musical utterance, right or wrong, becomes in time a self-fulfilling prophecy.

Herbie Hancock recalls the time Miles Davis heard him play a wrong chord and responded by simply playing his own solo around the "wrong" notes so that they sounded correct, intentional, and sensible in retrospect. Jazz musicians assume that you can take any bad situation and make it into a good situation. It's what you do with the notes that counts. Instead of engaging in traditional problem solving, Davis simply said yes to the notes that were in front of him with the assumption that he could make something work.

In a similar vein, pianist Don Friedman noticed after the fact that he had played the wrong chord during a recording session with trumpeter Brooker Little. Like Davis, Little responded by brilliantly shaping a solo around the alleged mistaken notes:

> *Little apparently realized the discrepancy during his solo's initial chorus, when he arrived at this segment and selected the minor third of the chord for one of the opening pitches of a phrase. Hearing it clash with the pianist's part, Little improvised a rapid save by leaping to another pitch and resting, stopping the progress of his performance. To disguise the error further, he repeated the entire phrase fragment as if he had initially intended it as a motive [sic], before extending it into a graceful, ascending melodic arch. From that point on, Little guided his solo according to a revised map of the ballad.*[2]

"Even when Brooker played the melody at the end of the take," Friedman observed, he varied it in ways "that fit the chord I was playing."

Note that Little did not try to fix blame or search for causes of the mistake but simply accommodated it as material to query for possible direction. He seized Friedman's error and made it sound intentional in retrospect through transformation, redirection, and unprecedented turns. Jazz improvisation assumes that there is affirmative potential waiting to be discovered from virtually any utterance, any chord, any note.

This is an example of what critic Ted Gioia terms an "aesthetic of imperfection."[3] Rather than grade the success or failure of individual creations based on some external standard of perfection—such as one might find with a classical musical performance—Gioia argues that with jazz, there is a need to evaluate courageous efforts. Such an aesthetic would involve evaluating the entire repertoire of actions that the musician attempted, the beautiful phrases combined with the clunkers that were the result of risky efforts, the same expansive efforts that no doubt produce beautiful passages.

Is an "aesthetic of imperfection" possible within organizations as well? I would argue that it's not only possible, but necessary. Too often, managers create monuments to organizational breakdowns by exhaustively searching for causes and by framing mistakes as unacceptable. Rather than encouraging brave experiments outside the margins, they immobilize the very people they are counting on to move the enterprise forward. Imagine, instead, a standard for organizational evaluation that assessed performances not just on conventional standards of success, but on strength of effort; level of purposeful, committed engagement in an activity; perseverance after an error has been made; and passionate attempts to expand the horizon of what had been considered possible. At the very least, such a standard would distinguish among errors that are the result of carelessness or disinterest, errors that are the result of systemic patterns (such as the six-sigma efforts), and those that emerge from caring deeply about a project. We might call the latter "noble failures."

Similarly, once errors are made, how do managers turn these unexpected events into learning opportunities, as imaginative triggers and prompts for new action, just as Davis did in the earlier story? Consider an example from the department store Nordstrom, which encourages employees to "respond to unreasonable customer requests." One Nordstrom employee paid a customer's parking ticket when the store's gift wrapping took too long.

A small example, but stories like this circulate and inspire other employees to use mistakes as an opportunity to provide enhanced service. In one memorable instance, a Nordstrom customer arrived at the store only to find that the suit he expected to pick up hadn't been tailored yet. He expressed his disappointment to the salesman, noting that he was planning to wear the suit at an upcoming meeting in Phoenix. Two days later when he arrived at his Phoenix hotel, a package was awaiting him—from Nordstrom. In addition to his suit, there was a letter of apology from the employee. But that's not all. Also enclosed was a matching shirt and tie. Little surprise that this customer continues to shop at Nordstrom and encourages others to do the same.

Instead of simply rewarding managers for "fixing" problems, organizations might apply their own "aesthetic of imperfection," considering not only the end result but also the way managers persevere and use mistakes as a point of creative departure, the same way jazz musicians branch off into unexpected directions from a few bad notes. This aesthetic implies that errors would be framed not as character blemishes, but as unavoidable mishaps to be creatively reintegrated as negotiation proceeds.

This also suggests that members within organizations must be willing to release one another for consequences that they could not predict, for errors of trespassing and overextension. Philosopher Hannah Arendt noted that the one antidote to the predicament of unpredictability is forgiveness. Imagine executives developing dual aesthetics of imperfection *and* forgiveness, advancing ad hoc action and serendipitous learning, while also releasing those who make noble efforts even when they don't achieve desired results.

## Taking Advantage of Errors

Business literature is filled with examples of innovations in organizations that actually depend on prior mistakes, and for very good reason: it's almost impossible to distinguish which ideas are going to succeed and which projects will lead to genuine innovation. Thomas Edison, so the story goes, tried and failed with hundreds of versions of the light bulb before he was able to invent one that worked. Each one of the failed attempts was necessary, as he and his colleagues built on what they were learning. For Edison, saying yes to the mess meant continuing to experiment even in the face of almost continual disappointment.

The story of Post-it Notes at 3M is an oft-told example of what can happen in a culture that celebrates ongoing experimentation. The development of "low-tack," reusable, pressure-sensitive adhesive was accidental—an error that proved to be a gold mine. Post-it Notes now generate almost 10 percent of 3M's revenue. Other examples of accidents that became unexpected opportunities abound: Pyrex cookware, Jello, Popsicles, the Walkman, Lifesavers, Coca-Cola, Silly Putty, Kleenex, Levi jeans, Band-Aids, corn flakes, penicillin, and many, many more.

In 1900, Lee de Forest was playing with batteries, spark-gap transmitters, and electrodes in his Chicago apartment when he noticed that the flame of a gas burner changed colors as he experimented with the spark-gap machine. Puzzled by the phenomena, he launched a series of failed experiments, tinkering and doing multiple iterations until he happened upon the triode that would become the basis of the vacuum tube—a critical element of radios, television sets, and ultimately digital computers. Even when he "succeeded," though, de Forest was working under the erroneous notion that the gas flame could detect radio signals.

In his account of de Forest's discovery, science writer Steven Johnson writes that one way to tell this story is that de Forest's life is an example of ingenuity and persistence.[4] But, he goes on, "telling the story that way misses one crucial fact: that at almost every step of the way, de Forest was flat-out wrong about what he was inventing. The Audion was not so much an invention as it was the steady, persistent accumulation of error . . . Even de Forest himself willingly admitted that he didn't understand the device he had invented. 'I didn't know why it worked,' he remarked. 'It just did.'" Johnson says it pointedly: "The history of being spectacularly right has a shadow history lurking behind it: a much longer history of being spectacularly wrong, again and again. And not just wrong, but *messy*."[5]

Saying yes to the mess allows you to notice details that you might have missed, while framing an inquiry as a problem or an experiment as failure kills curiosity. Consider the example of Wilson Greatbatch, a hobbyist who had been tinkering with electronics and radio signals. As part of a project with the psychology department at Cornell University, Greatbatch found himself working on a farm, measuring animal brain waves, heartbeats, and blood pressure with an assortment of instruments. At lunch one day, he overheard two physicians talking about the health risk associated with their patients' irregular heartbeats. Given his interest in electronics, he began to imagine the heart as an organ that gives and receives radio signals.

Now, fast-forward five years, and Greatbatch is working at a chronic disease institute in Buffalo, helping a physician put together an oscillator to record heartbeats. Steven Johnson picks the story up from there:

> One day while working on the device, Greatbatch happened to grab the wrong resistor. When he plugged it into the oscillator, it began to pulse in a familiar rhythm. Thanks to Greatbatch's error, the device was simulating the beat of a human heart, not recording it. His mind flashed back to his conversations on the farm five years before. Here, at last, was the beginning of a device that could restore the faulty signal of an irregular heart.[6]

Greatbatch and a Buffalo surgeon named William Chardack went on to develop the first implantable cardiac pacemaker and deploy it in the heart of a dog. By 1960, the Greatbatch-Chardack pacemaker was pulsing steadily in the chests of ten human beings. In the five decades since, variations of the original design have given a new lease on life to millions of people around the world.

Like so much great jazz, Greatbatch's pacemaker is a story of bricolage, of tinkering, combining disparate material (radios and hearts), iterations of errors that accumulate into a hunch that has lasting value. A simple mistake—pulling the wrong resistor out of a bag—and a willingness to stick with it long enough to connect the pulse of the oscillator to that overheard conversation about irregular heartbeats half a decade earlier and his own curiosity about whether the heart was a radio that emits signals led to an invention that has done untold good. But what is it about such "errors" that often lead to new discoveries?

Perhaps the answer is that errors violate expectations. Essentially, they disrupt routines and unthinking behavior. They wake us up and demand that we pay attention to something that previously was in the background. We are forced for the moment to look again, to become curious, to ask about our own approach. We have to disengage ourselves from patterns and pay attention in new ways. An error can energize us to investigate strange outcomes and can lead us to discovery. When we make a mistake, it's not possible to comfortably live inside our assumptions and comfortable beliefs. We're forced to confront our biases; we have to explore alternatives. Jazz improvisers and great scientists and innovators alike know the value of keeping at it: making guesses, trying things out (sometimes repeatedly), tinkering with incremental adjustments, all with an open spirit of curiosity and wonderment.

The invention of Play-Doh is another case in point. Noah and Joseph McVicker made wallpaper cleaner that produced a smudge goo. Smudge goo is used to attach wallpaper to hard surfaces. When the demand for wallpaper started to decrease, Noah needed to do something with the excess goo. Fortunately, his sister, a nursery school teacher, noticed that the goo was similar to modeling clay. She suggested they give it to the kids to play with, and it was an immediate hit even though originally it came in only one dull color: off-white. Later, they created several colors, began to market it through department stores, and went on to sell 900 million pounds over the next fifty years.

## Constructive Failure

In entrepreneurial ventures, not only is trial *and* error rampant, it is essential, as is a tolerance for the mistakes that are made. In fact, more than any other single factor, what distinguishes Silicon Valley as the innovation capital of the world may be the way entrepreneurs, engineers, and technologists treat their failures. Randy Komisar, CEO of the famous venture capital firm Kleiner Perkins Caufield Byers, says that Silicon Valley is a "culture of constructive failure."[7] Here, too, examples are abundant.

Apple is renowned today for the iPod, iPad, iPhone, and other breakthrough market successes. People forget, though, that the Apple Newton was a massive failure, but one that Apple built on to create its later successes. It was a constructive failure, as was Omega, a database program that technologists at Microsoft spent years developing, only to earn a big, fat goose egg in the marketplace. But here again, the skills and knowledge that engineers developed working on this failed project were later indispensable when they created the highly successful Microsoft Access. Microsoft also invested significant resources in trying to create a joint operating system with IBM, another big disappointment, but that led to the Windows NT system. Several failed attempts to create a spreadsheet that could compete with Lotus 1-2-3 eventually resulted in the development of Microsoft Excel.

Google, too, can point to a long list of constructive failures on its way to building a market cap in the trillions of dollars. One failure is almost funny in retrospect. Despite its name, Google Video originally didn't allow for viewing videos—which turned out to be the very first feature that users asked for. So Google immediately set to work getting the rights to play videos and developing a good player for the browser. To Marissa Mayer, Google's vice president of search products and user experience, it's less the error than the aftermath that matters.

*People would say "Oh look at Google, and there's all these innovative things" and they remembered the high points and they say "Have you ever made mistakes?" And the answer is we make mistakes every time, every day, thousands of things go wrong with Google and this product. But we launch things and iterate really quickly, people forget about those mistakes. They have a lot of respect for how quickly you build the product up and make it better.*[8]

But you don't get to the kind of positive aftermaths—that is, constructive failures—I have been describing in this section without a mind-set that values innovation and understands that ideas need time and resources for incubation. Google expects all employees to spend 20 percent of their time on some creative idea other than their day-to-day responsibility. This is an enormous leeway to experiment and pursue intuitions and inklings, and also a vital expression of what James Brian Quinn calls "controlled chaos"—a mix of stability and instability, planned and unplanned change, control and autonomy.[9]

## Making It Safe to Keep Trying and Learning

On first blush, a jazz quartet might seem to have little in common with, say, an assembly line or the cockpit of a commercial airliner. Jazz encourages riffing. The best performances rarely repeat themselves. As we've seen, jazz players don't correct mistakes so much as they recognize and ride with them. If the pilot on a New York-to-Chicago flight finds himself a few degrees off course and decides to follow his bliss to, say, Dallas, *no one* inside the plane or out is going to be happy. Nor are assembly line bosses likely to encourage experimentation on the job. Manufacturing organizations need to operate with efficiency and precision, the seeming opposite of jazz's mantra of serial creativity.

Yet both types of organizations are complex learning systems. (I'll say more about this in chapter 4.) Both exist in environments that are error-prone by their very nature, and both are at their best when they treat errors not as high crimes and misdemeanors but as essential learning opportunities. So for both types of organizations, one of the principal duties of leadership is to ensure that people learn from mistakes rather than hiding them or glossing over them.

Like a well-run factory, the U.S. Navy is organized to maximize efficiency and reliability, but when teaching officers to steer a ship, the navy is not all that dissimilar from a jam session. Several junior officers and one or more senior officers are on the bridge. As the junior officer is learning to steer, the senior officer issues corrective orders publicly, in the presence of the entire group. Thus, shared learning occurs even though no one calls explicit attention to the fact and on the surface no one even seems to notice that it's happening. The junior people who haven't yet had a chance to assume greater control—that is, solo—are learning about errors and how to correct them. Meanwhile, the senior people are learning what kinds of errors are likely to happen, how to best educate to avoid them in the future, and how to share information in a way that benefits not only the operator but also those who someday will be called to the same role.[10]

Hospitals are another high-reliability, high-risk environment in which mistakes inevitably happen, mistakes that are sometimes a matter of life and death. In 2000, the Institute of Medicine reported that anywhere from 44,000 to 98,000 people die each year in American hospitals as a result of errors. Mistakes with less dire consequence are, of course, far more extensive in hospitals than most care to admit or want to know. The traditional remedy to guaranteeing patient safety and well-being is through the training and performance of doctors and nurses. However, researchers such as Harvard Business School's Amy Edmondson have suggested that it's also critical to build organizational cultures that enable people to learn from mistakes. Edmondson and others argue that, given the unavoidable failures in complex systems, developing an organizational capacity to learn from these mistakes is a strategic imperative.[11]

For Edmondson, the biggest enemy to exploring learning is the pressure to pretend that mistakes didn't happen. People need to feel safe enough to talk about their mistakes. There needs to be a sense that the team allows members to take interpersonal risks. Do team members respect each other and hold one another in high regard? Do team members feel secure enough so that others will not rebuke, marginalize, or penalize those who speak up or challenge common practices or prevailing opinions? When there's enough psychological safety, people openly confront and discuss errors.

Sometimes there's irony to such cultures. When Edmondson was doing research on nursing teams in hospital emergency rooms and operating rooms, she looked at those units that had the highest independent ratings in terms of leadership and the health of the organizational culture. The bottom line: the healthiest teams with the strongest leadership reported more errors. At first, Edmondson assumed there was a mistake in the data entry. How could this possibly be the case? Several more trips through the data, though, confirmed the finding: the teams reporting more errors were actually the ones with the *strongest* cultures and best leadership. Edmondson explored further and ultimately found that in these teams, leaders expected people to report on and discuss errors. But more importantly, beyond leaders' expectations, let's appreciate the impact—the actual behavior of the employees and the benefits to the system. The employees did report errors and they learned from them. The actual numbers of reported errors may have been higher, but the actual errors were lowered because people learned from one another and were willing to admit and grapple with mistakes, rather than bury them.

As important as it is to treat errors as teaching opportunities, it's equally critical to build a culture in which people feel comfortable admitting and discussing their mistakes, and that requires leveling status differences. Substantial research shows that the biggest obstacle to creating the psychological safety that allows people to learn from mistakes is a hierarchy. When those with status are distant or intimidating, those beneath them are more likely to save face by hiding or ignoring errors.

In her book *Teaming*, Amy Edmondson describes three scenarios. A nurse has misgivings about the medication that is being given to one of her patients, but is hesitant to call the doctor. A copilot does not speak up when he sees a warning sign. An on-the-rise executive doesn't express reservations about a planned takeover or swallows his own reservations about what he suspects might be a pyramid scheme because the partners above him seem gung-ho for it.[12] The examples are plentiful, and often tinged with pain. In his bestseller *Outliers*, Malcolm Gladwell notes that Korean Airlines have more plane crashes and hypothesizes that in Korean culture status is highly regarded, making it harder for someone to speak up and challenge an officer higher in the hierarchy. It's a culture in which one is expected to be deferential toward elders and superiors and Gladwell shares examples of incidents in which the copilot knew the plane was in trouble but did not speak up to his superior.[13]

"When individuals learn, the process of trial and error—propose something, try it, then accept or reject it—occurs in private. But on a team, people risk appearing ignorant or incompetent when they try something new," Edmondson writes in *Speeding Up Learning*.[14] To overcome such hierarchical impediments, Edmondson and her fellow researchers advocate what they call a "fallibility model"—team leaders who might say, for example, "I screwed up. My judgment was bad in that case."[15] Even with open-heart surgery, cardiac teams led by a "learning leader" who fostered "a learning environment by admitting [his or her] mistakes to the team" were most successful in adopting a new surgical technique (in this case, minimally invasive cardiac surgery) and performing it effectively. One surgeon Edmondson cites told his team on several occasions: "I need to hear from you because I'm likely to miss things."[16] Such moves by high-status leaders go a long way to creating a culture of psychological safety.

Conversely, failing to use errors as a source of learning and to flatten status distinctions often indicates organizational inertia. Max Bazerman and Michael Watkins argue that organizations that fail to learn from errors become vulnerable to predictable surprises. Sim Sitkin ties the seemingly innocuous unwillingness of organizations to embrace small contemporary mistakes to larger failures to respond to future crises.[17] In a well-documented example, Robert Ulmer, Timothy Sellnow, and Matthew Seeger found that "many of the flaws in NASA's organizational culture that led to the Challenger disaster reemerged in the Columbia crisis" a decade and a half later, even after "dramatic changes in leadership, shuttle structure, and communication procedures were enacted to remedy problems found during the Challenger investigation."[18]

## The Perils of Perfection

The late Oscar Peterson was (and still is) the most fluent jazz pianist I have ever heard and still a personal favorite. I've already mentioned how shocked I was to discover, as I moved more into the jazz world, that while Peterson was widely admired, he was not well loved. Those incredibly complex licks played at amazing speed and with great virtuosity came at a great price as far as many of his peers were concerned. Instead of stretching himself beyond his own comfortable limits and pushing the edge of competence, Peterson settled for the impossible: perfection.

It was only later that I understood why this may have been the case. First, Peterson had been trained as a classical pianist, by a teacher who was a student of the virtuoso pianist Franz Liszt. Classical musicians seek practice as a way to achieve flawless execution. That was part of it, but there was another reason that might have made it even harder for Peterson to risk too much in public settings. He had been enormously successful at a spectacularly early age. He had won a national piano competition in Canada when he was only fourteen. A decade later, still a tender twenty-four, he was discovered by the great jazz impresario Norman Granz, who arranged for him to play in a concert as part of the famous "Jazz at the Philharmonic" series at Carnegie Hall. This was the pinnacle of the jazz world. Shy of his twenty-fifth birthday, Peterson was playing jazz with the greatest jazz musicians of his day—Dizzie Gillespie, Lester Young, Roy Eldridge, and others—and he was playing in one of the most famous classical music halls in the world. With a background like that, no wonder he found it so hard to risk making a mistake in public.

I thought of all that a few years back when I heard tenor saxophonist Sonny Rollins play at Ronnie Scott's, a legendary jazz club in London. Rollins, as I mentioned earlier, is often considered the greatest living improviser. His commitment to continually attempting something new and fresh, even beyond his comfortable limits, is legendary. One result of such boundless experimentation: Rollins sometimes stinks. I can't say he smelled the place up completely in London, but I went on successive nights, and Rollins sounded like a completely different player on the two occasions. I knew the song he was playing; it was a standard. But he played in ways I had never heard before, and at first I struggled to make sense of it. Later I realized that he was stretching the limits of harmony within a standard song. There were mistakes, to be sure, but there was a world of learning to be found in every one of them.

Jazz musicians often learn "fallibility models" from their teachers. They talk about provocative learning relationships that model surrendering to possibility rather than defending enactments. Trumpeter Wynton Marsalis grew up under the tutelage of a master pianist who happened to be his father, Ellis Marsalis. On one of Wynton's recordings, he asked his father to play piano. According to Wynton:

> *My father's so much hipper than me and knows so much more, but I can tell him, "I don't like what you played on that," and he'll just stop and say, "Well, damn, what do you want?" Then I'll say, "Why don't you do this?" and he'll try it. That's my father, man . . . If I said I didn't like it, he'd change it, and at least look for something else, because he's a sensitive musician. The more I get away from him, man, the more I know how much I learned from him just by looking and watching. I grew up with one of the greatest examples.*[19]

That exchange is a microcosm of a provocative learning relationship that nurtures an aesthetic of openness and surprise. In this situation, Wynton apparently has musical insight that he thinks is harmonically more appropriate than the chords the pianist (his father) is playing. Upon hearing the bandleader's (i.e., the son, Wynton's) suggestions, Ellis (the father) does not defend the correctness of his musical ideas, or generate rationales to explain his choice, but immediately respects his son's suggestions.

Who is the learner here? This is an excellent example of overcoming status barriers to create a learning moment. Ellis might seem to be the pupil, trying different musical ideas, but upon further inspection, another kind of learning is happening as well. Father is teaching son about a non-defensive, open approach to inquiry, and Wynton seems to walk away with a lasting insight, admiring Ellis's approach to and immersion in music, as well as his openness to learning and commitment to creative invention. The young Wynton was learning that even established, admired musicians must be willing to abandon comfortable practices and to abdicate postures of established status that block the emergence of good ideas—a useful lesson in any field of endeavor.

## Risk Taking in a Safety Zone

Granted, errors happen in any complex system. Granted, also, that no one should be overjoyed by screwups. (The word alone says it all!) But what happens when you build a psychological safety zone that accounts for imperfection and allows for experimentation and perhaps erroneous response? Consider this fairly mundane but telling example from my own permanent turf: the Naval Postgraduate School in Monterey, California.

My colleague Ted Lewis runs a very successful executive development program on our campus. Several times each year, a group of top managers flies in from around the world to take an intensive course taught by faculty Lewis pulls together. The execs arrive on Sunday and take two full weeks of classes. Generally the sessions roll happily along without incident, but not always.

A few years back—just as one of Lewis's new sessions was about to launch—a 4 a.m. bomb scare closed the campus down tight. Lewis learned about this when he checked his computer at 7:30 that Monday morning and, not surprisingly, started to panic. There were thirty-four executives at a local hotel who would be coming to campus in one hour, only to find the place in lockdown mode. Several faculty members had flown in as well, and they weren't likely to be any happier than his nearly three dozen corporate high flyers.

Concerned (too mild a word), Lewis got on the phone and called his secretary, Mary Lou Johnson; her line was busy and he felt panic blossoming. He waited a few minutes and tried again, he later told me, and that's when he found out why her line was busy. Johnson had learned about the bomb scare an hour and a half earlier. In that ninety minutes, she had called a local hotel conference center and reserved an empty conference room. She also had rented audiovisual technology and other materials, including flip charts and markers, seen to it that the conference room was arranged in a classroom setting, secured transportation to the conference center, sent a notice to the hotel where the executives were staying with instructions to the new location, and notified the executives themselves. At 8 a.m., when the faculty arrived at the makeshift classroom, students were seated and ready to begin. Lewis was more than pleasantly surprised by the bold initiative his secretary had taken to make all these arrangements without notifying him or asking his permission. In fact, he was thrilled.

What made it possible for Johnson to know that she could take these initiatives? Lewis never gave her explicit permission to do a single element of the quick turnaround. Nowhere in her job description were such expectations spelled out; indeed, it would be impossible to spell out such unforeseen obstacles and challenges in advance.

But in a large way, that's the point. By word, but mostly by deed and example, Johnson was *free to respond to the demands of the situation.* She would not have been able to do so had she been obsessing about the fear of failure.

In some contexts, we might think that she went out on a limb by making bold decisions without checking with her boss, and to be sure, some bosses would have been extremely displeased that they had been kept out of the loop. Some bosses might have sent a signal throughout the organization that they needed to be informed. Some would fear public embarrassment. But in this case, a largely unspoken trust between the leader and the members of the organization created a safety zone in which Johnson was tacitly empowered to act when action was most needed. Looking back on it, Lewis said, "I realized that I know things are going well when I'm the last one to know."

What if Johnson had misjudged? What if the bomb scare had been called off and the campus reopened in time for the class to meet as scheduled? There was no guarantee of this, and we have to appreciate that Johnson was taking a big risk. The cost of the rental and the transportation was significant, and the department—like virtually all academic departments these days—was facing budget constraints. Instead of a heroic act, Johnson's frantic scrambling for a new venue could have gone down as wasted money in a department where resources were indeed tight. Even then, though, her efforts would have amounted to a noble failure—Sonny Rollins on a bad night, say—as opposed to a disinterested shrug of the shoulders. Better to have loved and lost, as the old saying goes, than never to have loved at all.

But the story also says something important about the culture and leadership that allows people in the middle and lower levels of an organization to do what Johnson did. She could have avoided responsibility and handed the mess off to someone else. It wasn't her fault after all, and nowhere in her job description did it say that she should make rearrangements in case the campus was in lockdown. However, in this department, leaders communicated the importance of serving the customers and providing an excellent educational experience; the organizational structure was minimal and allowed people maximal autonomy to do the right thing; there was strong agreement that it's important to serve the customers; people were appreciated for creative efforts; people told stories about times others responded to unexpected and unusual demands. All of these messages won the day, and it probably never entered Johnson's mind that she was overstepping her boundaries.

## Venturing Forth in the Midst of Peril and Excitement

Wouldn't it be nice if complex systems were simple and error-free? If fallible humans were infallibly perfect? If the workplace and business world generally knew nothing of violent eruptions and stormy seas? Not really. The fact is, people often learn best when venturing forth in the midst of peril and excitement, deeply immersed in the activity at hand. Research has shown that when people are fully engaged at work, they are more committed to contributing to the effectiveness of the organization. William Kahn calls engagement "the harnessing of organizational members' selves to their work roles; in engagement people employ and express themselves physically, cognitively, and emotionally during role performances."[20]

The standard characterization of the competent manager portrays him or her as a detached observer—analytical and dispassionate— safely removed from the immediacy of conflicts in order to handle challenges objectively. When novel, challenging situations arise, leaders are "expected" to not lose their cool and to seek an analytic explanation. The action is inside the mind: management is a process of noticing discrepancies, stepping back and analyzing them, and working through the puzzles intellectually. In practice, though, detached intellectual analysis usually means that people ask familiar questions, generate standard classifications, and produce predictable answers.

Relying upon a detached mind-set is far more likely to bind to established routine than lead to breakthrough insights.

Jazz musicians, by contrast, often speak of letting go of deliberation and control. They employ deliberate, conscious attention in their practice, but at the moment when they are called upon to play, this conscious striving becomes an obstacle. Too much regulation and control restricts the emergence of fresh ideas. To get jazz right, musicians must *surrender* their conscious striving. This they do by deliberately facing unfamiliar challenges, by developing provocative learning relationships, and by creating incremental disruptions that demand experimentation and risk. In the words of saxophonist Ken Peplowski: "You carry along all the scales and all the chords you learned, and then you take an intuitive leap into the music. Once you take that leap, you forget all about those tools. You just sit back and let divine intervention take over."[21] Peplowski continued:

> *When we play at our best, I find many times that I'm not actually thinking about anything and you can actually have a strange experience of going outside of yourself and observing yourself while you're performing. It's very strange. And you can actually listen as you're playing and listen to the rest of the group, and you can be completely objective and relaxed. And come to think of it, completely subjective also, because you are reacting to everything else around you.*

This is what I mean by leaping in and taking action. The best jazz players court disaster. They actively pursue not control, but its opposite—that moment of surrender to the music and all its possibilities, good and bad, when "nothing is left of you but a purposeless tension," in Peplowski's phrasing. They are totally in and of the moment. To return again to a favorite side subject of mine, by risking so much, jazz musicians achieve what Kierkegaard, in his essay *The Present Age,* called "essential engagement."

Kierkegaard was writing specifically about the press—about how it had removed discussion and interaction from the face-to-face venue of the coffeehouse to the impersonal pages of newspapers and journals, and made it possible for people to form and offer opinions from a safely detached distance, absent any sense of personal responsibility. We've now moved beyond the printed word, but what Kierkegaard had to say applies equally to our own time. "The Public is not a people, a generation, one's era, not a community, an association, nor these particular persons, for all these are only what they are by virtue of what is concrete. *Not a single one of those who belong to the public has an essential engagement in anything.*"[22] To become a full human being, Kierkegaard believed, we must commit to action, practice new skills, and put ourselves at risk of public failure. Only through such full engagement is a meaningful life possible.

Perhaps that's why, unlike the idealized office manager, jazz players are anything but detached. If you look at photos of jazz musicians playing their instruments, you see individuals fully immersed, completely absorbed in their playing. When Keith Jarrett is improvising jazz, he is so of the moment that he can often be heard moaning.

Indeed, over the years, I've noticed that some of the world's best professional photographers are enamored of jazz musicians. Why are they so drawn to musicians playing their instruments? I think one reason is that jazz musicians are so deeply engaged in their playing. They are fully immersed in their music, attached to their instruments. Photos of Bill Evans, for example, show him playing the piano hunched over, deeply immersed in his playing, as if he wants to become part of the piano. In the photo, you can't tell where the piano ends and Evans's body takes over. Look at Stan Getz playing tenor sax, and you'll see someone who appears to be in a transcendent state. Bass player Ray Brown has an expression of ecstasy as he leans over his instrument. This is full engagement, and the only way to get there is to lay everything on the line.

Although he doesn't mention moaning, professor Lee Fleming's detailed description of Hewlett-Packard and its success in inkjet printing provides an example of an organization leaping in and taking action in several "high variance inventive trials" to create "technological turbulence." HP exploited some of its existing knowledge but mostly engaged in rapid prototyping and testing—what Fleming calls "a repeated and continuous process of recombinant search" and a "stream of inventive episodes"—to achieve technological breakthroughs in inkjet printing.[23] The two key HP inventors, John Vaught and Dave Donald, "considered and built numerous combinations of inks, resistors, slides, electrodes, explosives, lasers, and piezo-electrics" before developing the final product.

Vaught described a portion of the inventive process in January 1979:

> *My first thoughts for a design were quite conventional . . . but before the parts got out of the shop I conceived of a pair of electrodes using the ink between them as a resistor to vaporize a small portion of ink very near the end of the tube thereby ejecting a droplet. We built such a device and Dave provided the electronics to drive it. It failed because we couldn't get the resistivity of the ink low enough to produce enough heat and it also produced hydrogen and oxygen at the electrodes. New idea! Let's produce a small spark between the electrodes and ignite the bubbles to eject the drop. It worked!*
>
> *One small problem, we couldn't produce the explosive mixture of gasses rapidly enough to meet the 2 kHz vision. Oh well, let's just put all the energy required for vaporization in the spark and forget about hydrogen/oxygen explosions. It worked! About this time we got permission to turn the gravure printing investigation into an ink-jet investigation. Finally, we were out from under the table. Dave and I life tested this version and got two days operation at 2 kHz before it failed which was not nearly long enough. Electrode erosion was the culprit. Then came the idea of a small resistor on the inner wall of the capillary to provide the energy necessary for vaporization. All this time Dave is strongly urging me to enter all these ideas in my lab notebook; what a waste of time I argued.[24]*

Even after they got the inkjet printer to perform as they wanted, admitted John Meyer, one of the engineers working on the project, "it wasn't clear at an elementary level how it actually worked."[25]

Vaught sounds very much like a jazz musician both in his relentless tinkering and tolerance for mistakes, and in his fundamental restlessness with the status quo. "I bore easily," he told Fleming, but "HP Labs was a wonderful place: I had to work in a single field for only two or three years and then like magic it was a whole new field, a paradise for creativity."[26]

Meyer also closely echoes the jazz aesthetic when he says of the entire team of inventors, "we were very much *involved* during this time, ideas were flowing freely back and forth, people were doing things in one area and other people working on different aspects of it, it wasn't compartmentalized [emphasis added]."[27] When the manufacturing team set out to build its own prototype print head, the process was so rapid that team members ended up punching the inkjet orifice by hand, using a sewing needle borrowed from an engineer's wife. Meanwhile, inspiration came from everywhere, including the coffee percolator on Vaught's desk:

> You think of things that are totally unrelated . . . Inventors just don't go home and see it at that moment in time. It is something that has happened way back in time. Due to a lot of things. As near as I can recall the percolator [inspiration] . . . it wasn't [rising] bubbles, if you think about it, if you left the top off, it went poof, poof, poof and blew gobs of coffee all over the place. When it comes to the moment of truth, you think about a lot of things.[28]

The HP story is also particularly relevant because it demonstrates that breakthrough innovations do not have to come from outsiders. HP was an established firm that was also successful in creating breakthrough innovation internally. Fleming argues that what allowed the HP inkjet team to innovate so successfully was the diversity of its membership: "It is less likely that the engineers from a purely mechanical or purely electrical engineering firm would have thought of or built such crazy combinations, simply because they would have lacked access to or inspiration from such a wide variety of readily available components."[29]

The Palo Alto–based design firm IDEO is famous for producing a number of creative products in a range of industries, including household, commercial, and industrial products and services. IDEO invented the computer mouse, the Neat Squeeze stand-up toothpaste tube, the Polaroid i-Zone instant camera, the thumbs up–thumbs down on TiVo's video recorder, and on and on. Arguably, no other company does a better job of learning about customers' needs and designing new products to meet those needs. But at the heart of IDEO's success, according to founder David Kelley, is this same imperative of diversity. The company draws employees from diverse backgrounds, including MBAs, electrical engineers, software designers, and linguists. What matters less is the training and field than the ability to think way outside the box. Kelley refers to the employees as "crazies" and "weirdos," proud of their deviance. They look at issues from a variety of angles, and according to Kelley, this is the source of their creativity. They leap in and throw out ideas, play with a myriad of material, and get physically involved by creating material prototypes, testing them out, destroying old ones and building new ones.

In this highly collaborative yet intentionally varied environment, employees become like cultural anthropologists, inquiring into the world of the users, engaging in deep empathy. They essentially do field research, then regroup and share what they noticed through intense brainstorming sessions. Kelley calls the process "focused chaos"—a phrase equally applicable to Keith Jarrett's performances. But it's not only the chaos that brings jazz to mind. It's also the sheer energy released by the diversity. Four saxophonists playing together could never embrace one another's errors the way, say, a single saxophonist working with a drummer, pianist, and trumpeter can forgive imperfection and make of it something transformative. Whether the field is jazz or business, that's innovation at its very best.

## CHAPTER FOUR

# Minimal Structure– Maximal Autonomy

## Balancing Freedom and Constraints

Jazz bassist and composer Charles Mingus once famously said, "You can't improvise on nothing. You gotta improvise on something." Musicians need a song, a motif, a set of notes on which to embellish and create an improvisation, and they're not alone in feeling that way. One of the greatest actors of our generation, Robert De Niro, famous for inventing brilliant scenes on the fly, argues that actors need constraints of character and situation in order to meaningfully improvise. Improvisation, in short, needs rules and some kind of order.

Jazz improvisation is a complex system. Information flows freely yet is restrained, members are diverse yet conform and remain richly connected, constraints are minimal, and feedback is nonlinear. Given that there are many possible responses to given stimuli and that the responses themselves can stimulate unexpected behavior, such a system is a good candidate for the development of novelty: tiny changes can amplify and alter the state of the system, escalating into qualitatively different patterns. Jazz bands are "chaordic systems," a combination of chaos and order. The critical design element for jazz bands and for leaders is the nonnegotiable constraints that need to be in place so that chaos can lead to creativity rather than something undesirable.

Jazz players look for and notice instability, disorder, novelty, emergence, and self-organization for their innovative potential rather than as something to be avoided, eliminated, or controlled. Indeed, jazz bands are very much human systems living at the edge of chaos. To understand their social complexity requires cultivating an aesthetic that values surrender and wonderment over certainty, appreciation over problem solving, listening and attunement over individual isolation.

We have been socialized in the other direction: to assume that systems need hierarchy to organize and have some stable order. Mechanistic forms of organizing feed the belief that the individual leader is the most important factor in keeping an organization on track.[1] But the emphasis on strong individual leaders and hierarchy doesn't end there: in an effort to guarantee consistency and efficiency, organizations often attempt to systematically avoid changes and ambiguity through creating standard operating procedures, clear and rationalized goals, and forms of centralized control.

Studies of complex adaptive systems, however, offer another model and suggest that systems are able to achieve coherence and order without any controlling leader or central authority. Ants, for example, follow very simple rules to build very elaborate colonies. Order is emergent, and ants achieve a dynamic equilibrium without an independent monitor or director. Similarly, order emerges without a central planner when termite colonies adjust delicately to one another and are able to produce cathedral-like mounds. Ants and termites are useful analogues to help us consider the systemic dynamics of emergent order without a central organizer. But ants, termites, and birds operate on instinct, not mindful adaptation. Human improvising involves another level of complexity.

When jazz is at its best, that same orderless order is at work. Players are in a continual dialogue and exchange with one another. Improvisers enter a flow of ongoing invention—a combination of accents, cymbal crashes, changing harmonic patterns that interweave throughout the structure of the song. Musicians are engaged with continual streams of activity: interpreting each others' playing and anticipating based on harmonic patterns and rhythmic conventions, while simultaneously attempting to shape their own creations and relate them to what they have heard.

Members have enough shared awareness of the common task and of each other so that they can monitor individual and group progress on an ongoing basis, but they're not burdened by demands of excessive disclosure or too much input to process. Each player brings a unique perspective to the enterprise, and there's enough disagreement and variety so that each utterance can be interpreted from a different point of view—in fact, the same person could easily interpret the same musical input differently on a different night.

As we saw earlier, the goal of each jazz performance is to find a groove, the state in which the players successfully achieve a mutual orientation to the beat. In a sense, the groove acts as what Donald Winnicott calls a "holding environment," a reliable nesting that provides a sense of ontological security, a place of trust that allows people to take risks and initiate actions.[2] As drummer Charlie Persip puts it, "when you get into that groove, you ride right on down that groove with no strain and no pain—you can't lay back or go forward. That's why they call it a groove. It's where the beat is, and we're always trying to find that."[3]

How is this magic possible? How does jazz work? How are musicians able to integrate, to start and stop together, to play within the same harmonic patterns, to coordinate and support each other, to create novelty, to respond in real time to one another with no blueprint, no explicit advance plan, no central controller or hierarchical authority? The answers to all those questions lie in both freedom and vigilance. Players are *free* to create novelty but also *vigilant* in their responsibility to attend to one another. Amid all of this freedom, the music remains coherent and yet not frozen. This is how improvisation occurs. It also gets to the very nature of complexity.

## Complexity Science: Emergent Self-Organization

The sciences of physics and biology were the first to articulate the dynamics of complexity theory, claiming that systems are so complex and interdependent that reductionist, linear thinking is inappropriate for understanding them. These scientists studied how nature evolves and came up with novel arrangements in which self-organizing principles transcend the properties of their parts, allowing small changes to have large consequences. In these arrangements, actions emerge when *disequilibrium* is reached, not when traditional order is achieved. Such complex adaptive systems are nonlinear and thus cannot be explained solely by dividing up and analyzing the parts.

The notion of complex adaptive systems has since migrated into the management and leadership literature. Meg Wheatley, Ralph Stacey, and others have written about alternatives to mechanistic, top-down control models, suggesting that we take seriously the notion that complexity theory proposes: *that systems are most creative when they operate with a combination of order and chaos.*[4] When systems are at the edge of chaos, they are most able to abandon inappropriate or undesirable behaviors and structures and discover new patterns more suitable for changing circumstances.

Under the Wheatley, Stacey et al. model, organizations are encouraged to value diversity, change, and transformation rather than predictability, standardization, and uniformity. Executives, too, are asked to notice and value instability, disorder, novelty, emergence, and self-organization for their innovative potential rather than as something to avoid, eliminate, or control. A new vocabulary that highlights fragmentation and marginality yields a more positive attitude toward elements once considered inconsistent with the purpose of organized, goal-directed activity.

While provocative, these suggestions have often been prescriptive rather than descriptive. The thinking is that we have few actual models of a human system living at the edge of chaos, making creative things happen. But as I argue in this chapter, we do in fact have one very human model to teach us how minimal structure can maximize diversity and autonomy in the service of creative results: jazz bands.

Jazz works because the process is designed around small patterns, minimal structures that allow freedom to embellish—a system that balances between the extremes of too much autonomy and too much consensus. So often we hear that good leadership involves creating consensus for how to proceed. One way to think about jazz is that it *minimizes consensus* around core patterns and allows diversity to flourish. When jazz bands are jamming, creativity is enhanced precisely because emphasis has been placed on coordinating action with consensus, disclosure, and structures, all reduced to the simplest levels. Modest structures value ambiguity of meaning over clarity, and preserve indeterminancy and paradox over excessive disclosure. These minimal commonalities are the simple resources that allow players to elaborate in complex ways, balancing autonomy and interdependence.

In jazz, improvisation is coordinated around songs, themselves made up of patterns of melodies and chord changes, marked by sections and phrases. Songs follow loose, tacit rules that allow innovation. When musicians improvise, it is usually based on the repetition of the song structure. These guiding structures are nonnegotiable, impersonal limitations: musicians do not have to stop to create agreements along the way. Musicians, for example, know the chord changes to "All of Me" or a twelve-bar blues, which is why players who have never met are able to "jam" and coordinate action.

These moderate constraints serve as benchmarks that occur regularly and predictably throughout the tune, signaling the shifting

context to all involved. Everyone knows where everyone else is supposed to be, what chords and scales players are obliged to play within.
Such minimal constraints allow them freedom to express considerable
diversity—transforming materials, intervening in the flow of musical
events, and even altering direction.

Once there is a mutual orientation around the basic root movement of the chord patterns, even the chords themselves can be altered,
augmented, or substituted. Songs and chord changes impose an order
and create a continuous sense of cohesion and coordination: all the
players know where everyone is at any given moment, and thus, individual players are able to innovate and elaborate on ideas with the
assurance that they are oriented to a common place.

The harmonic changes are anchored by the bass. Bass players have
a foundational role as coordinators. They play the pulse and, especially when they are walking through the changes, are outlining the
harmonic framework. Bassist Cecil McBee explains: "It's important
that the player understands that his musical position is to ascertain
the pulse, the harmony and rhythm all in one. He's the heartbeat . . .
What I mean is *all* are listening to him, all are listening to that pulse,
that sound for guidance. The harmonic path, the rhythmic-harmonic
pulsative path that the bass takes serves as a guide toward whatever
improvisation . . . is to occur at the time."[5]

The irony here is that by defining the chordal movement, the bass
player allows the pianist to play what are referred to as "harmonic
substitutions," not the standard, predefined chords. When pianists
embellish and extend the chords in novel ways, they make the music
more interesting, suggesting alternative voice leadings and pathways for the soloist, who can now play around and outside those
changes, to create novel lines and to depart from standard formulas
and respond in novel ways. This can also have the opposite effect. If
the bass player is not listening to how the pianist is extending and
embellishing the harmonic outline, the pianist must accommodate
the bass player.

Rhythm also allows players to coordinate while diverging, a seeming paradox that is central to the jazz aesthetic. When the feel of the rhythm is strong and reliable, soloists can take greater risks and play "out of time," knowing that they can land back in the groove. Manage this tension well, and the music becomes very innovative. Drummer Ralph Peterson explains:

> When you're playing a solo—rhythmically—what the notes say . . . [is] almost as important, if not as important, as the notes themselves, because if you miss a note and the rhythm is logical, then the idea comes across . . . whether you hit the note dead center or not. But if you miss the time—because music is organized sound in time . . . if you blow the time, you're more likely to do irreparable damage to that particular section of the music.[6]

In the final analysis, three components of minimal structure of songs allow jazz players to coordinate:

- Jazz musicians work within clear, nonpersonal constraints, that is, they do not require interpersonal trust. Players know that they need to orient their choices within a certain range of notes that fit within the chord or the scale, but they don't have to stop and negotiate or debate which constraints are worth attending to. They simply trust that all the players will adjust to the patterns. In effect, they employ detached, impartial trust, another seeming oxymoron that goes to the very core of the art form.

- Once the constraints are set, players engage in lots of interaction and communication around these minimal patterns. They share ongoing information and adjust to what they hear. The chord changes come around each verse, but they are suggestive and open, waiting to be fully realized. People persevere, trade motifs, engage in spirited exchanges, and support one another to take off and embellish in one or more directions within the framework of the small rules.

- Critically, too, these constraining patterns are punctuated, occur at regular intervals, and follow a temporal rhythm. Coordination is made possible because of the punctuated coming together that allows a going apart, convergence, and divergence. Because these constraints change each measure (or each beat), these nonnegotiable structures invite dialogical engagement. In the space between these "check-ins," everyone is able to embellish and branch off in unpredictable directions, in search of fresh meanings.

In his new book, *Permanent Emergency*, Kip Hawley, the former head of the Transportation Security Administration, recounts an incident from earlier in his career when he was serving as vice president for reengineering at Union Pacific. No point was more critical to the railroad's success than the Powder River Basin of Wyoming—Union Pacific transported coal from there to power plants throughout its system—and no point was more difficult to handle.

> *Because on-time performance from this one spot was so valuable and important—a serious delay in delivery could black out the entire city of Atlanta—Union Pacific spent enormous resources trying to improve efficiency. We rushed high-priority coal cars to a continuous queue just outside the single-point entry to the basin. We advanced new empty cars right after the previous train moved out. But instead of maximizing efficiency we were actually overdoing it . . . As with brain surgery, there was no room for error.[7]*

And error, of course, was exactly what happened, time and again. Finally, after reading James Gleick's *Chaos*, Hawley writes that he had an epiphany. Instead of queuing up the high-priority cars so one delay was sure to affect all of them, the railroad would distribute them far more loosely throughout the system and flow them as needed.

By easing up instead of further tightening down, Union Pacific increased its daily coal-car count by 30 percent.

"By accepting errors, we created a much more robust system," he writes. "Loosening our grip a bit made our whole system stronger and less vulnerable to a high-impact event like a broken locomotive or a landslide—errors that would be catastrophic in an over-regulated control environment."[8]

This is exactly what jazz does.

## Fostering New Ideas and Creating New Products and Services: Design and Prototyping

In organizations, what would be the equivalent of structures that are minimal, nonnegotiable, and impersonal in the sense that participants tacitly accept rules that do not need to be constantly articulated? How can organizations achieve fluid coordination without sacrificing creativity and individual contributions?

Karl Weick suggests that one organizational equivalent of minimal structure might be credos, visions, slogans, mission statements, and trademarks.[9] Organizational slogans such as FedEx's "The World—on Time" or its earlier motto, "When it absolutely positively has to get there overnight," are catchy phrases awaiting embellishment, encouraging individual members to elaborate on this version of jazz's melodic path. In the spirit of minimal constraints and minimal consensus, keeping such phrases ambivalent actually becomes an organizational strength, because doing so leaves the phrases open to multiple and perhaps contradictory interpretations. There can be *too much clarity* in organizations. Excessive specification of requirements and expectations can limit an employee's imagination and thus capacity to respond in the moment. Mottos like FedEx's are action-opening, launch-pad structures suggesting pathways and responses to situations that could never be anticipated in advance.

Or consider the role of organizational stories and myths and how they elicit creative responses from people. Stories such as that of the Nordstrom employee who paid a waiting customer's parking ticket act like the chord changes of a song. Each time a customer appears to be treated badly, such stories persist as markers to remind and seed other employees with ideas to embellish on the melody, initiating unusual actions to satisfy clientele.

These same principles apply to coordination in projects and new product development. Managers too often pay disproportionate attention to beginnings and endings. They put structures in place to launch a project. Due and delivery dates become all consuming. But there's rarely much talk about coordination in real time once a project begins. Sedimentation creeps in. People get immersed in their own worlds, so that when someone alters action or changes direction, no one is sure where others are located, what other changes they have made, and what adjustments they themselves should make. As a result, they either feel too constrained to take creative action or, when they do, discover too late that they have caused massive problems for others. Every jazz combo has sessions like that—sometimes you never find the groove—but no one looks forward to evenings like that.

One organizational route to the equivalent of the successfully improvised song might be rapid prototyping, including regular updating and design change. Such a practice would almost compel cross-discipline communication so that people could create while knowing how and where their ideas fit into the whole evolving system.

That's basically what Kodak did when it created the FunSaver camera more than two decades ago. Rather than working separately, the engineering, manufacturing, and marketing departments created a shared workspace and collaborated to develop a prototype for the camera. Designers made changes and creative contributions to their individual parts, but would also regularly update the schematic for the whole camera. Each morning, these individual changes were made public and accessible so everyone saw the results of their joint efforts on an ongoing basis and each member knew where everyone else was through every stage of the design.

Today's computer technology can enhance that process even more. Instant and constant public access to changes and other contributions allows everyone involved to stay attuned to the possible direction, like changing the root movement of the chord. People add variants—like the drummer adding accents—that might inspire creative departures. Rapid prototypes function like the loose framework of the song. They leave a great deal of room to depart and deviate, and yet there is enough structure to give players sufficient collective confidence to play together. The temporal updating of the minimal structure notifies everyone where others are in their incremental innovations and increases the likelihood that people can achieve successful joint awareness throughout the life of the project.

## Innovation and Guided Autonomy

By saying yes to the mess and valuing the art of improvisation, leaders can create the conditions for *guided autonomy*: identifying the limited structures and constraints that facilitate coordination around core activities. This means maximizing opportunities for diversity rather than insisting on unity or too much agreement. By hedging against the trap of "too much consensus," leaders give subordinates additional freedom to experiment and respond to the sort of hunches in which true innovation is often found.

Dov Frohman and Robert Howard write about this often deeper challenge of management in their book *Leadership the Hard Way*: "The goal of a leader should be to maximize resistance—in the sense of encouraging disagreement and dissent. When an organization is in crisis, lack of resistance can itself be a big problem. It can mean that the change you are trying to create isn't radical enough . . . or that the opposition has gone underground. If you aren't even aware that the people in the organization disagree with you, then you are in trouble."[10]

Too much consensus is just as dangerous as too little. The trick is to have enough agreement through time so that individuals and groups are free to embellish, branch out, and do something wild and creative, knowing how and where others are oriented. When I'm playing jazz, I can't know for sure what someone else is playing in the ninth measure or what's going to happen. But for certain songs, I know that the song will be in the general vicinity of a D-minor chord, and that gives me enormous freedom. Too often in organizations leaders think that if they get the three Rs clear—rules, roles, and responsibilities—innovation will logically follow. More often than not, results go 180 degrees in the opposite direction.

Wikipedia, the open-source, online encyclopedia that launched in January 2001, is a highly prominent example of innovation not by structure but by guided autonomy. Founded by Larry Sanger and Jimmy Wales, Wikipedia was originally intended to be a feeder line of sorts to Nupedia, an already existing online encyclopedia edited by acknowledged experts. Constraints are few for Wikipedia—anyone can submit. Structures are minimal—links can carry a single entry in almost infinite directions. Rules remain largely tacit and impersonal, and riffing is commonplace. Readers, for example, are constantly invited to "disambiguate" articles, which can lead to further "disambiguation," and on and on. "Accuracy," in consequence, is always a bit of a moving target. Someone somewhere—in fact, many people many places—is always mad at Wikipedia: the facts are off, the emphasis wrong. But the dissent itself is part of the creative process, part of the impetus that keeps the encyclopedia dynamic. And the overall result on the information superhighway has been nothing short of miraculous: a collection of more than 15 million articles, free to the public and globally accessible in more than two hundred languages.

Free and open-source software—that is, software that can be freely copied, modified, and reused in any fashion—has a similar and much deeper history. In the early days of computing, virtually all software was freely shared. Beginning in the late 1960s, though, a succession of court cases and industry practices increasingly sequestered software use, and by the early 1980s, the vast bulk of software was available only for sale.

In 1983, Richard Stallman of the MIT Artificial Intelligence Laboratory began the pushback against commercialization with his GNU Project of free software. Nine years later, Linus Torvalds released his Linux kernel, a freely modifiable source code that quickly attracted volunteer programmers, just as Wikipedia quickly attracted volunteer encyclopedia contributors. As with Wikipedia, structure remains minimal and constraints few with the Linux kernel. Torvalds "guides" the autonomy. Contributors of necessity have to pay homage to where the code has been—to paraphrase Charlie Mingus, "You can't innovate on nothing"—but the code itself is in a constant state of creation, just as is the case with jazz.

## Loose Coupling and Dynamic Capability

A jazz combo wears its minimal constraints on its sleeve. Players are free to transform materials and intervene in the flow of musical events, altering the direction of the piece. Once there is a mutual orientation around the root movement of the chord patterns, even the basic chords themselves can be altered, augmented, or substituted.

With other organizations, the process can be harder to spot, but the effect is much the same. A healthy group typically shifts from tight to loose coupling over time. Coordination is not achieved by static rules, but through the evolution of ties between participants, allowing for the emergence of surprising detours. There is strong enough interdependence to complete tasks and bring ideas to fruition, but the ties are not so tight as to be suffocating.

One example of a firm that has demonstrated dynamic capabilities in such a loosely coupled context is Omron, a $7 billion,

35,000-person global Japanese manufacturer of sensors, control system components, advanced electronics, health-care devices, and related services. Omron's "song" is its deep-rooted, globally defined principles.

In an interview with my colleague Ethan Bernstein, CEO Hisao Sakuta specifically identified the Omron Principles as one of the company's most important strategic structures—a singular commonality that connects all activity within the firm. Asked how one set of principles could possibly unite people across dozens of different geographies, languages, and cultures, Sakuta pointed to the minimal nature of the structure imposed by the principles and how that openly encourages improvisation around them:

> Whenever I speak with employees, I tell them their interpretation of the Principles should not be a set answer. Please be true to your own personal understanding and how you can express it, using the language of the Principles. We have 35,000 employees, and I think it's perfectly fine for there to be 35,000 different understandings of the Principles . . . No matter how different the workplaces are in terms of race, value sets, geographical locations, etc., as long as we can continue this common debate and discussion, we are able to maintain a flexible attitude to respond to any changes to come in 50, 100, 200, 300 years. And I believe we will be able to refine the Principles by doing so.[11]

Some leaders would try to force universality and compliance, putting in place structures to ensure strong governance across a global footprint. Instead, Sakuta uses the minimal structure of the principles—not how they are written, but how they are interpreted—as his governance structure. The result is maximum autonomy for localized innovation that has produced a steady flow of major innovations, including advanced sensor technologies to prevent counterfeiting on high-resolution color copiers, auto systems that automatically apply the brakes prior to an accident, and improved food safety through the deployment of biosensors capable of automatically detecting if food is harmful (past date, diseased, poisoned, etc.) if ingested.

Toyota likewise understands that dynamic capability means mastering minimal structures. Toyota operates on four simple rules:

*(1) All work shall be highly specified as to content, sequence, timing, and outcome; (2) Every customer-supplier connection must be direct, and there must be an unambiguous yes-or-no way to send requests and receive responses; (3) The pathway for every product and service must be simple and direct; and (4) Any improvement must be made in accordance with the scientific method, under the guidance of a teacher, at the lowest possible level in the organization.*[12]

Those simple rules provide the minimal structure necessary to avoid chaos on a fast-moving factory floor. Outside those rules, ordinary workers are given maximum autonomy to constantly improve their methods and suggest improvements elsewhere. They have mastered the art of learning while simultaneously executing for efficiency.

Bernstein witnessed all this in action during a recent tour of Toyota's Tsutsumi plant.[13] He was watching the installation of the center console on the third-generation Prius when a bottleneck in the process triggered a full line stop three times in short order.

As problems mounted, more and more supervisors came over to investigate the problem. In many manufacturing environments, such breakdowns in the manufacturing line would have immediately risen up the hierarchy. Why? Because managers are more capable of handling exceptions and unusual events. That's what supervisors do—they handle the messy breakdowns, removing solutions from the purview of the line worker.

At Toyota, though, the four simple rules in effect allow line workers the autonomy to address unusual challenges within their immediate sphere of execution. In this instance, supervisors did not tell the operator what to do. To the contrary, the supervisors provided support to get the line moving again, thus freeing up the operator to solve the problem by adjusting the tooling facility to make the installation smoother. This was all done in seconds, even as the line continued to move.

Similar to IDEO's policy of allowing employees to design their own workspaces, Toyota allows its operators to design their own tools, workspaces, and processes. The result: seamless processes that almost resemble a dance in the most unlikely of places—a factory floor. Toyota achieves thousands of such dances, leading to extraordinary throughput and quality by providing operators with minimal structure and maximum autonomy. When supervisors get involved, they bring expertise and extra hands, not autonomy-squelching structure.

Investments in minimal rules that free employees to meet challenges by deviating from normal practice are investments in organizational learning. Encouraging employees to try something else when breakdowns occur might produce nothing more in the short run than incremental change, but by institutionalizing the principle of minimal nonnegotiable rules, companies are fostering a metacapacity for improvisation and organizational change. What jazz bands, Omron, and Toyota have in common is a jazz mind-set that supports dynamic capabilities. They are able to explore and experiment with novel ideas (autonomy) while still staying loyal to essential routines (structure).

## Guided Autonomy and Group Dynamics

To see how guided autonomy can filter down into the infrastructure of an organization, consider the following experiment in group dynamics conducted by an Omni Hotel in the Midwest. This organization had been a traditional bureaucratic structure with an authoritarian management style in which employee and managerial turnover was unusually high and morale strikingly low. For years, interdepartmental conflict and turf wars had kept the departments from creating coordinated strategic direction. The top management group in particular had a history of conflict. Discussions were often bitter and defensive. Members of two departments in particular were highly suspicious of one another, and discussions often led to polarized, monologue-like spirals of indignation and self-righteousness.

When the general manager, who had been reading about organizational theory, set out to create four-star service, the top hotel and restaurant rating from Michelin guides, he knew that the major challenge would be to create a culture of interdepartmental cooperation and participative management. To that end, he began holding group meetings with his top twenty managers to discuss the direction of the hotel. Discussions, as anticipated, often had a competitive tone that worked against cooperative agreements. Some members even refused to speak to one another.

After the managers met for a four-day, offsite, strategic planning retreat, they formed three task forces to address core strategic issues. One came back to the larger group with a proposal for strategic action that would require cooperation of all the warring departments. The underlying idea was to nurture employee empowerment and participation throughout the organization, an action that radically challenged the current cultural norms. The subgroup members knew that simply voting on the proposal would not lead to committed action and indeed was likely to solidify already warring positions around turf issues. Further, having debated the idea among themselves for two months, they knew there were various sides to the issue that were legitimate and that they needed to address. Was there a way to voice these perspectives without linking them to individuals who then might feel obliged to defend their views?

With the help of a consultant, a strategy emerged: the subgroup set up three tables in different corners of the room. Each table was labeled with an index card that "marked" the various perspectives—like the chord changes of a song—that members would speak from. The task force leader then introduced the activity:

> *Obviously this is a big deal. It would represent a major change for*
> *employees and managers if we took this course of action. We want to*
> *talk about the implications of the proposal, but rather than simply vote*
> *on this or ask if you want to do it, we need a chance to voice all of the*
> *perspectives and implications. We have set up three tables around the*
> *corners of the room, and we have put index cards on each. The cards*
> *are titled according to the point of view we would like the subgroups*
> *to discuss: (1) support for the proposal; (2) against the proposal; and*
> *(3) concerned about the implications of this proposal. We would like*
> *you to not immediately go to the corner that best represents your own*
> *opinion at the moment. Try picking a viewpoint that is a stretch for*
> *you and surface ideas from that perspective.*

For thirty minutes, each of the three groups discussed the proposal in an energetic and lively fashion. When the whole group came back together to dialogue about the proposal, they were not asked to report what their groups had discussed but simply to talk about the proposal. The ensuing exchange was remarkable. Not only were people less compelled to defend old positions, subgroups traditionally divided were talking more freely and sometimes even found themselves articulating one another's traditional views. After an hour of dialogue, the group agreed to adopt the proposal on a six-month trial basis.

What made this approach transformative for this particular Omni management group? One key factor certainly was the willingness to improvise within the minimal constraints of the "song" the task force had created. Participants were willing to suspend moral judgment based on personal histories or turf protection. They could support the development of alternate approaches (including some they might have normally found repulsive) because they knew that, in the end, a wide array of ideas would be legitimately voiced and supported.

And they had learned along the way that somewhere in that array of utterances was one with the potential to lead to somewhere the whole group wanted to go, as happens with a good jazz solo.

## Unbuilding the Unthinkable: Coordination Through Minimal Structure

More than a decade later, the attack on and subsequent collapse of the World Trade Center towers on September 11, 2001, still remain almost unthinkable. The thousands of lives lost; those haunting images of commercial airliners being turned into weapons of mass destruction; the raw bravery of firefighters, police, and ordinary citizens who kept trying to rescue those caught in the towers even as they were starting to tumble down—all that will live in the national memory for untold generations. But there's another side to the 9/11 cataclysm that demands equal attention in its own way: not the destruction, but the cleanup that followed.

As outlined in William Langewiesche's book *American Ground: Unbuilding the World Trade Center*, this is a story of a remarkable accomplishment. Never before had anyone seen 1.5 million tons of ruins from seven big buildings covering seventeen acres. The volume alone was mind-boggling—how does anyone or anything deal with 1.5 million tons of twisted steel, cement, and the remains of three thousand people? But this was an extremely dangerous site in more ways than one.[14]

Under the ruins of the North Tower, for example, was whatever survived of the main chiller plant—one of the world's largest refrigeration units, responsible for air-conditioning both towers. Contained inside the unit were roughly 168,000 pounds of pressurized Freon, a toxic chemical containing chlorofluorocarbons (CFC). Diesel excavators could easily puncture the CFC containers. If the CFC leaked, it could infiltrate the pile and suffocate the workers. Worse, if the Freon ignited, it would turn into hydrochloric acid and phosgene gas, similar to the mustard gas used during World War I. Langewiesche writes: "Everyone knew that if the Freon came hunting for you at the center of the pile, you would succumb."[15]

There were other obstacles as well, including emotional outbursts and conflicts between firefighters and police. Some firefighters, in fact, seemed to be most concerned about their own people and not as interested when remains of civilians or police were recovered. Part of that was the special fraternity of firefighters: some had lost family members and nearly all had lost friends. Langewiesche notes also that society at large had expressed special support and sympathy for the firefighters, and "the emotionalism seemed to have heightened the firemen's sense of righteousness and loss."[16]

This, then, was the situation: highly volatile and backbreakingly complicated. And yet, in the end, not a single life was lost in the cleanup, and the job was completed $700 million *under* budget and nine months *ahead* of schedule. How did this happen?

Langewiesche writes that the traditional approach to managing such a crisis would have involved lengthy preparation:

> *In other countries clear answers would have been sought before action was taken. Learned committees would have been formed, and high authorities consulted. The ruins would have been pondered, and a tightly scripted response would have been imposed. Barring that, soldiers would have assumed control. But for whatever reasons, probably cultural, probably profound, little of the sort happened here, where the learned committees were excluded, and the soldiers were relegated to the unhappy role of guarding the perimeter, and civilians in heavy machines simply rolled in and took on the unknown.*[17]

As Langewiesche suggests, the 9/11 cleanup is a story not of overmanagement but of a group that coordinated with no prior plan, no clear organizational structure or chain of command, no rich experiences

to help make sense of this unprecedented event, and no collaborative experiences. The World Trade Center was "unbuilt" by disparate
actors, many of whom did not get along, working from different bases
of expertise with no routines to rely upon, and no bureaucratic structure or clear authority to turn to. Like a common practice in jazz,
most of these players met for the first time on 9/11.

In the midst of all the mess and all the horror of 9/11, one man
leaped in and, in effect, said yes to the mess. Mike Burton was a
construction manager and engineer who officially bore the title of
executive deputy commissioner of the New York City Department
of Design and Construction (DDC). The agency is responsible for
the design, construction, and repair of New York's public buildings,
including police stations, fire stations, and public libraries, as well as
roads, sewer projects, and water mains. The DDC was not tasked to
respond to city emergencies and was certainly not designed to super-
vise disaster cleanup. That work, one might have assumed, would have
fallen to the city's more prestigious Office of Emergency Management or to a federal agency such as the Federal Emergency Management Agency (FEMA).

Burton happened to be attending a meeting in lower Manhattan on the morning of 9/11; otherwise, Langewiesche notes, Burton
would not "have had any reason to get involved in the recovery from
the disaster."[18] But this was a dynamic situation and proximity counts.
Burton's car was stuck in traffic, so he pulled over and began walking to the towers. Even when the first debris storm hit, he continued
moving toward the site. Within a few hours, Burton was directing the
response. Within a few weeks, he was directing a workforce of over
three thousand. Over the next ten months, he would coordinate a
hundred thousand people from a multitude of different agencies.

At first, Burton had no real idea what to do, so he began simply
making calls. He initially didn't comprehend that both towers had
completely collapsed, so his first call was to a scaffolding company. As
Langewiesche reports, Burton assumed that there would be falling

glass and he needed to protect people from the debris, so he called a scaffolding company and asked them to "prepare to load a half mile of sidewalk bridging onto their trucks."[19] He had imagined that there were hundreds of people trapped and suffering in the ruins and they needed to be pulled out. In retrospect, it seems a silly miscalculation—there were no "structures" left—but Burton had created a momentum that would grow and grow.

Knowing that heavy equipment and crews would be needed, Burton ignored the "legal" bidding procedures and called four construction companies he was familiar with, "the first that came to mind" companies that had earned reputations because of prior work with the city—AMEC, Bovis, Tully, and Turner—and asked each of them to send representatives to a meeting at police headquarters. All four companies would soon secure lucrative contracts to clean up the site, but all improvisation entails risk, and this was no exception. Because the four companies did not go through the normal bidding process and had not secured prior insurance, they were exposed throughout to possible claims and lawsuits.

Simultaneously, Burton was calling around to mobilize an assessment team, a collection of fourteen engineers and contractors who would accompany him as he made his first walk through the site that evening. Like a stone in a pond, those calls sent ripples heading to the far banks.

Ironworkers just started showing up. The contractors started calling in subcontractors and equipment, and soon a collection of construction specialists were working around the clock. Eventually, Port Authority engineers and fire department experts in building collapse joined the core group. FEMA provided federal money.

Burton and his DDC boss, Ken Holden, soon set up an emergency command center in a nearby public school kindergarten classroom. At first, they held nonstop meetings with representatives from a list of city, state, and federal agencies and worked around the clock.

To keep communication flowing, Burton created a minimal structure for temporal updating—regular, twice-per-day meetings—one in the morning and one in the evening. For both daily meetings he and Holden would be in the classroom; everyone who wanted to know what was happening or had something to share was to send a representative to the meeting. There was no time for planning. As Burton put it at the time, "there's no time for distributing memos or waiting for the chain of command. Everybody has to hear what the problems are. The decisions have to be made, and everybody has to hear those decisions. We have to keep everybody moving in the same direction."[20] To make sure there was enough psychological safety and to encourage honesty and so that people could speak up freely, there was a ban on all electronic recording equipment.

"Within 72 hours," Langewiesche writes, "they had gone from chaos to managed chaos, with a more organized management structure, and a more sustainable schedule: a 24-hour, seven-day operation with three 11-hour shifts."

Eventually, twenty government agencies were represented at the twice-daily meetings. Most people were wearing construction overalls and boots. They sat around on windowsills and kindergarten desks, clustered around the room. It was important people could speak frankly and honestly. The idea was to allow participants to propose ideas that might seem foolish at first blush and to swallow their pride when criticism was directed their way. At these meetings, Langewiesche writes, "There was a new social contract . . . all that counted about anyone was what that person could provide now."[21]

Meetings alone weren't giving the cleanup team the necessary data. They needed to learn about the pile. To get there, Burton imposed an initial semblance of order by dividing the huge pile of debris into four parts and assigned each of the contractors to one of the quartiles. What was the logic for dividing the pile into four? As Langewiesche points out, "The four-quadrant pattern owed as much to the presence of the four companies . . . as to a compelling operational logic, but while it endured, during the first urgent months, it functioned reasonably well."[22]

Burton also imposed simple operating rules for his own interface with the debris piles. If he heard noise coming from each quartile of the pile, he knew that progress was being made. When he stopped hearing noise, he treated this as an anomaly that required his direct attention.

"No one ever asked us to do it, no one ever told us to do it," Burton said of the four-pile arrangement, "but in retrospect, when they saw things happening, they knew it was movement in the right direction." That, in fact, is generally true of the entire World Trade Center site cleanup. At no point in the entire operation did anyone place Burton in charge of the cleanup effort at Ground Zero. He said later: "None of us wondered, 'Should we make contact with the state?' 'Should we contact the Feds?' . . . We had the equipment. We had the connections. We could handle it. We just went in and did what we had to do. And no one said no."[23]

By the terms of New York City's official and secret emergency plans, written before the attack, the Department of Sanitation should have been in charge of the cleanup. Indeed, there were dissenters all along the way who decried the lack of a binding chain of command, but in the real world of the cleanup, formal lines of authority went quickly out the window. After the first week, when an official from the city's Office of Emergency Management walked up to Burton and Holden and said, "Who told you to get involved?" they simply stared at the woman in disbelief and went about their work. As Lange-wiesche writes, "there was shift of power in their direction that *was never quite formalized and indeed was unjustified by bureaucratic logic or political considerations*" [emphasis added].[24]

Clearly, Burton's story demonstrates that leadership means taking risks, leaping in, and violating rules—all broad principles of jazz as well—but it also illustrates more specific tenets of the art form as it relates to minimal structure. Consider, for example, the following moments from Burton's story and their broader implications:

- *Burton began simply by making calls.* This is reminiscent of jazz players' starting their solo with "almost any group of random notes." Instead of searching for a path and then taking it, musicians learn to take action before the actual action paths emerge. They begin by groping, searching through the mess, working with the resources at hand—the chords, motives, riffs, *and* like Burton, the people who are around at the moment.

- *In retrospect, calling the scaffolding company seems like a silly miscalculation.* But from the perspective of improvisation, something else is happening here. By reaching out for resources, even when they were the wrong ones, Burton was experimenting with how to take action in an unparalleled situation. He was creating an identity, surprising even himself as he discovered he was capable of something he had not previously imagined. In jazz and in life, this is how you learn who you are and what you're capable of.

- *Knowing that heavy equipment and crews would be needed, Burton ignored the "legal" bidding procedures and called the four construction companies he was most familiar with.* Good improvisers have a knack for knowing when to break rules. Burton activated his network; he drew upon the people he had known over the years. This is bricolage in action—dealing with the available tools and resources, tinkering with what he had on hand, and combining resources as a way to proceed.

- *Dividing the pile into quartiles and assigning each one to a specific construction company* was like creating a jazz quartet. Burton was letting people loose to discover what they needed to respond to, where the priorities lay, and which problems they needed to address first. This move ceded maximal autonomy to the construction workers, while freeing Burton to create a mini-structure for coordination. (In contrast, consider what happened after Hurricane Katrina when the situation spun out of control while everyone was waiting for the authority structure to activate.)

- *Burton imposed simple rules and a minimal structure for coordination—regular, twice-daily meetings.* Just as happens with a jazz ensemble, the two daily meetings coordinated action through time, both allowing each player significant autonomy to respond as the situation required and also providing an opportunity to adjust to one another based on new information. Once these baseline understandings were in place, Burton and others were free to improvise.

Throughout the entire cleanup, but especially in the critical first weeks, Burton created small coordinating constraints that did not require interpersonal trust. Indeed, these players had never worked together before, and so did not have the luxury of experience that warranted trust. He created a forum so that the players could interact and share perspectives. During the recovery period, they shared lots of information that allowed the players to reframe and update their sense of what was going on. Finally, Burton created a minimal constraint that was punctuated and had a temporal rhythm, like the chord changes of a song. The parties knew that there would be an update meeting each morning and each afternoon in which all participants would share information and listen to what others were doing. Here, too, as almost everywhere else along the action chain, minimal structure created maximal authority to act.

Burton wasn't on a bandstand waving a baton. He was directing a cleanup under some of the most tragic circumstances in American history, but as any good jazz musician will recognize, he was also leading a song, in just the right way.

## CHAPTER FIVE

# Jamming and Hanging Out

## Learning by Doing and Talking

Jazz musicians live for the jam session. They love to play together, calling out songs for each other, and then hang out afterward to talk about the session and share experiences and insights. A special kind of knowledge transfer takes place during those sessions, one that can't be replicated in any other way.

I recall, for example, jamming at a local bar in Cleveland with saxophonist-clarinetist Ken Peplowski. He has amazing technique and range; he can play Benny Goodman solos as well as Charlie Parker and Sonny Stitt at high velocity. Often, he would call songs at a tempo that was simply too fast for me to play with any comfort, but that was the tempo Peplowski called. So I would give it a try, stumbling and fumbling through chorus after chorus until I found my own groove and became comfortable with speeds I never thought I could attain.

Over time, I became accustomed to Peplowski's playing and the songs he called, but guest musicians were always popping in to stir up the pot again. They would prefer songs that I didn't know and play in a style I was not familiar with, so the whole learning process would start over. Sometimes it was a disaster, such as when the saxophonist who had been listening to John Coltrane and learning all his licks called "My Favorite Things," a Coltrane-style standard in a minor key with odd rhythms and chord changes. He then followed with "Giant Steps," a song with very complex harmonic changes that he insisted be played at a breakneck tempo. I can still feel the discomfort in my stomach as I limped along, barely following the song. His solos made no initial sense to me, and afterward I asked Peplowski to make sure that he did not return. But the mad saxophonist did come back and called similar tunes, and eventually I grew more familiar with his style and could play through the changes of these strange songs. In that way I stretched myself in the same way that athletes stretch their talents, by stepping up to ever-greater levels of competition.

Every established jazz musician has at least one similar story to tell about "paying dues" at a jam session—being ignored or embarrassed in some way, but learning in the process. Charlie Parker is commonly considered the greatest jazz soloist of all time, but in 1936 he was playing in a jam session in Kansas City when the drummer Philly Jo Jones grew so impatient that he threw a cymbal at Parker's head—an experience that proved to be formative. Parker said that afterward he practiced fifteen hours a day for three or four years, learning standard tunes in all twelve keys. When he returned to performing in public, he was a different player.

Parker claimed that in the midst of one particular jam session in 1939, shortly after he got back to playing, he discovered a method of building solos based on chord changes and their extended intervals. These were intervals, he said, that he had been hearing in his head but had never been able to realize on his instrument. But playing in this jam session, he was able first to stretch out and try what he was hearing, and then to extend his solos into several chromatic extensions; this became the foundation of bebop improvisation. Out of his experience, Parker went on to write his classic song, "Ko-Ko," one of the most influential numbers in jazz history. These discoveries could not have happened were it not for the context of a jam session.

## Hanging Out

What made the learning process even richer was hanging out afterward. When the jam sessions closed down, we would go for a drink or for a meal at a late-night diner and talk for hours about the harmonic changes, the rhythmic displacements, the inspiring moments, the songs on which we connected and the times when we didn't connect, and on and on.

Here I learned about the importance of balancing autonomy and interdependence. I recall a bass player saying to me once, "You need to stop playing as if you're playing solo. It's making you play too many notes. You can rely on the bass more." That was priceless feedback and changed my playing forever. And I wasn't alone. Stanley Turrentine remembers that he learned from others by "asking about things I didn't understand." One young trumpeter even recalls learning how to dress from "hanging out" with Miles Davis.[1]

The stories that passed back and forth about jazz players we knew or had heard about were almost as valuable as the technical information that passed across the table at these late-night sessions. Here I learned about Charlie Parker's practice techniques, Thelonious Monk's idiosyncratic personality and how he approached rhythm, the courage of Benny Goodman in working with African American musicians in the segregated 1930s. I learned about the lifestyle of living on the road, the challenges of playing in places where patrons bought drinks for the musicians, stories about colleagues who experimented with drugs, and even a few tragic stories about jazz musicians who destroyed their lives with heroin and other addictions.

These sessions after the sessions were identity-creating moments. We were teaching each other about what it means to be a jazz musician—the sacrifices, the rewards, how to balance the challenge of the music life with family life, how to be a good sideman, what gigs to accept and which ones to reject, and so on. And it was also a time for honest and blunt feedback. This is learning of a different, deeper kind, and jazz musicians over the decades have clearly intuited that because they have built the spirit of jam sessions—stretching, sharing, helping—into multiple aspects of their lives.

Local communities of practice developed in the early 1950s around metropolitan areas such as Detroit, Chicago, and especially New York: as in jam sessions, players would hang out and draw knowledge from each other. Trombonist Curtis Fuller recalls how peers challenged and sustained one another through collaborative discoveries, attempting difficult technical passages or importing other kinds of music:

> I stayed at 101st street, and Coltrane was at 103rd street and every day I could just take my horn and walk around there—stay over there all day. We'd have tea and we'd sit and talk, and we'd laugh and put on records. Coltrane would say, "Hey Curtis, try to play this on the trombone." And I would try to run something down. I'd struggle with it and he'd say, "You're getting it" and so on and so on.
>
> Paul Chambers lived all the way in Brooklyn, and he would get in the subway and, gig or no gig, he would come over to practice. He got this thing—a Polonaise in D minor—and he'd say "Hey Curtis, let's play this one." It wasn't written as a duet, but we would run that down together for three or four hours. A couple of days later, we'd come back and play it again. The whole thing was just so beautiful.[2]

I've experienced this beauty myself: a special fraternity often develops among jazz musicians as they guide each other through obstacles and challenges. Whether the venue is jam sessions or a larger learning community, there's a spirit of serious playfulness, even safety, associated with this sharing. By playing together, people are learning to think differently, relate differently.

## Cognition and Social Processes

The Russian psychologist Lev Vygotsky was one of the first to notice that social interaction plays a major role in cognition.[3] We internalize the external voices of others that we hear around us, and this becomes part of our thought process. Lev Vygotsky considered thinking as internalized speech.[4] In other words, social learning precedes development. Relational exchanges precede cognitive growth.

Vygotsky challenged the notion of measuring intelligence as if it were a static thing that can be assessed. For Vygotsky, the critical issue is the "zone of proximal development," the gap between the current level and potential level of development. What's important is to cultivate experience and seek relationships with people who are within the zone of proximal development. Vygotsky argues that most learning, from childhood on, occurs in relation to others who are more skilled—parents, teachers, tutors, competent peers. *Scaffolding* conveys much the same idea: a teacher or competent peer helps the learner through the zone of proximal development and then gradually withdraws as the learner becomes more competent.

This doesn't apply solely to children. When adults have extended positive interaction with skilled peers, they develop a greater reflective capacity and expansion of skills. Good musicians, like competent executives, have *learned how to learn*. They know how they can achieve more when they hang out with supportive others who are skilled enough to be just beyond their own actual level of development.

Such an approach to cognition tends to fly in the face of traditional notions of education, which hold that people learn best not by social interaction but by being exposed to information: gathering data, registering it, and storing it in memory so that it can be recalled at appropriate moments. In this view, knowledge grows through logical, incremental accretion. This approach to learning gives special weight to analytic reasoning, a deductive process of a step-by-step ascension on a path toward objective truth. Knowledge is something that is acquired, like an object, and represented in the mind as a concept. This theory of learning is the logic behind many formal training programs in which concepts are delivered and people are expected to build up a storehouse of explicit knowledge and rules that will allow them to perform tasks.

As we saw in chapter 1, Paulo Freire calls this the "banking concept" of learning—knowledge is an object inside the head that can be transferred from one person to another, like transferring deposits from one bank account into another. Indeed, the banking metaphor spreads itself, at least implicitly, broadly across the literature of learning.

Think of some of the common phrases already used in this book: "knowledge transfer," "technology transfer," and the like. Advances in information technology in areas such as intranets, data repositories, and expert systems also lend themselves to thinking of knowledge as objects to be rapidly shipped from place to place, port to port, repository to repository. These innovations seem to hold out the promise of wider, more efficient distribution of lessons. The overriding assumption is that people are moving knowledge around and through the organization just as funds are electronically transferred and distributed.

In the same logical vein, the next step would seem to be capturing knowledge so that, like captured capital, it becomes available for others in the organization. Information technologists emphasize the need to collect, analyze, sort, disseminate, and apply information so as to create ever-greater effectiveness. Storing knowledge in histories, after-action reports, and other forms of memory also supposedly helps members learn and adapt to a constantly changing environment.

The antiseptic nature of such knowledge acquisition—would seem to be far superior and certainly far more predictable than the yes-to-the-mess, jamming, catch-as-catch-can education of most jazz musicians, but for my money, informality has all the advantage in this matchup.

Yes, certain tasks such as solving a calculus problem probably require a formal transfer of abstract concepts, but clearly many of the most important skills you can develop are not supported by this kind of cognitive process. How do you learn to be a carpenter? It is certainly not just a matter of capturing and memorizing categories and rules. Or how do you learn to ski? Think about a time you were learning to ski or learning to hit a tennis ball over the net. Books and instructional videos can only help you so much. You need to get out there, get the feel for the terrain or the velocity of the ball, and learn how to balance yourself. You learn as you do. But this same principle can be extended beyond sports challenges. How do you learn how to convince a colleague to dedicate resources to a change program? How do you learn to give feedback to an executive whose relationships with his senior team are suffering? Books with how-to lists can help to a point. But these kinds of skills involve engaged, absorbed activity and ongoing experimentation that goes beyond the learning of rules. Complex activities—jazz is only one—demand a complex knowledge set that can be gained only through experience. This type of higher knowledge is very personal, rooted in action, ingrained and taken for granted, and not easily articulated, codifed, or stored.

## Human Capital: Learning as Banking

*Human Capital: The knowledge, skills, competencies and attributes embodied in individuals that facilitate the creation of personal, social and economic well being.*[5]

Sometimes I worry that just as we think of knowledge as an object, we actually start to think of people the same way. This, too, is in our language. The phrase *human resources* belies a certain bias toward viewing people as something that can be utilized, controlled, moved around, acquired, and dispensed with. But the language has recently been expanding in other ways. We hear references to "social capital," again as if relationships are objects that can be owned or wielded. When we say that someone or something "has lots of social capital," we're implying that relationships are possessions to be utilized, like hammers or tool belts. Combine the two into "human capital," and we end up treating humans, at least metaphorically, just as we treat other resources like buildings, technology, supplies, and cash—something that can be quantified and transferred.

Many organizations have designed executive education with a similar reliance on "capital" metaphors. They send executives to class where they listen to speeches or watch PowerPoint presentations from world-class experts—a model in which knowledge is represented and transferred to student learners.

Some years ago, I helped design an executive education program for the U.S. Navy. There were senior naval officers from around the globe and representatives from each branch of the fleet: jet aviators, surface warfare, submarine officers, supply officers, and medical corps. All of them had been brought to the Naval Postgraduate School specifically for this course on leadership.

The main designers put together several modules meant to maximize both time and information outflow. Sessions started at 8 a.m. every day, including Saturday, and featured a series of guest speakers—specialists in strategy, motivation, human resources, and change management, lecturing until 5 or 6 p.m. each day. On paper, the schedule looked awesome, but when I first saw how cramped it was, I wondered aloud if this amazing array of diverse specialists—men and women who rarely got a chance to speak to each other—was ever going to have an opportunity to learn from and about each other.

If ever there was a chance for inspired jamming and hanging out, it seemed to me this was it, especially in a military context, but the people in charge of the course worried that if they didn't fill the hours with classroom lectures, the senior officer at the Pentagon who was paying for the course would object. As one of the course designers told me: "We flew them all the way out here. We took them out of their day jobs. We have to use their time well and show that they are getting something. If it seems we are giving them lots of free time, it will look like a boondoggle and senior people will start to question why we're are doing this and why they should bother to support it."

At one point, I sat in the back of the classroom and counted how many PowerPoint slides the executives saw. The answer on that one day alone: over two hundred slides on various approaches to leadership. There was discussion, of course, but the discussion was usually questions and answers between the instructor and the students and only occasionally back-and-forth exchanges among the students themselves. In the end, everyone present—faculty, organizers, and attendees—got a ticket of one sort or another punched, but I'm guessing most of what was "deposited" in the brains of those attending had evaporated before the students had resumed their postings. I remember saying to myself, "This is a lost opportunity. This sort of thing happens every day in organizations. They need to break out of it because it's killing creativity."

## Adult Kindergarten: Learning as Play

Undoing, even reversing the mind-set that underlay the navy executive-training course I've just described led in some fairly extreme directions, especially in the heady days before the high-tech bubble burst, back at the start of the century. Formerly button-down, uptight

Big Eight accounting firms suddenly began launching "creative centers" where pretty much anything went. A colleague recalls one such venue, near a famous university:

> *The place was laid out to encourage congregation. Natural sunlight poured in on spacious landings with conversation pits, virtual jungle gyms (for the going-on middle-aged), and every sort of toy imaginable. A bright 5-year-old would have thought she'd fallen into her best dream ever. There was a communal kitchen that always seemed to be stocked with snacks, breakfast and lunch treats, even a bar for after-hours sharing stocked not only with mini-brew labels and better-than-generic wines but also with drinks so healthy they should probably be banned.*
>
> *I loved it! I thought this place was paradise, an idea incubator without equal. And then I began noticing that all those amazing spaces and gathering and play points were mostly empty. Yes, the architecture was inclusive, but the people weren't necessarily that. They clung to their wide-open offices and found ways to create psychological if not actual physical boundaries between all their spaces. In the kindergarten, everything was hunky-dory, but the bonhomie always seemed forced. In the real 9-to-5 world, it was every man and woman for themselves.*[6]

I don't want to idealize jazz or jazz musicians. I've known plenty of trumpet players, drummers, and saxophonists who, given a choice between their private space and a wonderfully designed public gathering space, would choose to be alone 90 percent of the time. But that, in a larger sense, is the point. The chance to come together is important; the space to make connections is vital. But the jamming I'm talking about, that late-night hanging-out, those communities of learning, can't be imposed by architecture or even forced by meeting planners or, for that matter, cruise ship social directors. Jamming happens spontaneously, whenever two or three or (best-case scenario) a dozen or more are joined in common purpose, common practice, and common desire to raise the bar for everyone involved.

That's what hanging around is really about: finding not only shared interests but the common groove that will bring people together so they can learn from each other and share the stories and experience that lead to meaningful breakthroughs.

## Designing *Real* Opportunities for Serendipity: Learning as Doing

To appreciate the value of bringing people together to learn from each other and share stories, recall the Xerox story cited in chapter 2. The company believed it could make copier service error-free by coaching representatives in every imaginable breakdown, and indeed, the plan worked fine until the machines refused to break in predictable ways. Finally, the problem was solved when the service rep and the technical specialist he summoned abandoned the diagnostic book. They began connecting this one anomalous breakdown to their own previous experiences and to stories they had heard from colleagues—exactly the way jazz musicians engage in absorbed, experimental learning that requires ongoing engagement and storytelling. In other words, learning by serendipity.

Many jobs require this type of improvisation—a patching together of bits and pieces of experience to cope with problems that don't provide definitive solutions. Manuals, standard operating procedures, and dictates from on high don't help us in these circumstances. It's only through conversing freely with others and storytelling that we fall upon possible solutions. Indeed, in Julian Orr's account of the Xerox repairmen, the process of forming the story becomes an integral part of the diagnosis.[7] This process begins and ends with communal understandings that are not available in standard documents; narration is an important element in integrating the various facts of the situation. Orr, in fact, stresses the dichotomy between managers' understanding of job requirements and actual practices: "Although the documentation becomes more prescriptive and ostensibly more simple, in actuality the task becomes more improvisational and more complex."[8] Bottom line: it's the storytelling that matters.

John Seely Brown and Paul Duguid refer to organizations by a term I've already used with jazz players: "communities of practice."[9] To foster learning, they contend, organizations must see beyond conventional, canonical job descriptions and recognize the rich practices themselves. Stories of past successes form a community memory that others can draw upon when facing unfamiliar problems. Similarly, Jean Lave and Etienne Wenger write about "legitimate peripheral participation," an acknowledgment that learning through naive questions, casual conversations, and offhand observations is legitimate.[10] Learning is much more than receiving abstract, acontextual, disembodied knowledge. Learning, in their formulation, entails knowing how to speak the language of the community of practitioners.[11]

In their classic study, *Situated Learning*, Lave and Wegner write at length about the apprenticeship model of education, in which (ideally) old hands pass on not only the skills necessary to a craft but also the culture, mind-set, and lore that underlie its practice. This is, of course, exactly what jamming is, but without the rigid hierarchy that guild and union apprenticeships so often enforced. With jazz jams, the learning and sharing can stretch out over an adult lifetime.

As old as it is, this kind of collaboration is still the way people learn, yet work is often designed with just the opposite in mind. Workers are isolated from one another, dampening and sometimes killing off the potential for collaborative learning. John Seely Brown, one of the key figures in the early days of Xerox PARC, tells a story that illustrates the importance of social process in learning new technology.

The new PARC employee was intelligent and hardworking, but she quickly got mired in difficulties with the office computer system.

The system came with the usual promises of user-friendliness, but she found it impossible to use or understand, and anything but friendly. As a newcomer, she was reluctant to keep asking for help, but suffering in silence seemed like a formula for having a breakdown.

The woman, Brown says, was close to quitting when her desk was moved from an isolated office into the center of a group of offices. There, she immediately benefited from the incidental learning that I mentioned earlier. She saw not only that these "stable" machines crashed for everyone but that there was no more "ease" for experienced assistants, longtime employees, or PARC's hallowed computer scientists than for her. And she also saw that when a machine did crash, its users would, without shame, look around for help from someone else who, whatever their status, had successfully steered around that particular problem. No one person knew how to handle these temperamental machines, but enough collective knowledge was spread around the office to keep them up and running.[12]

When we design work systems with no eye to collaboration, social process, and serendipitous discovery, we overlook multiple key resources. Brown writes: "The 'geek' who understands the network, the secretary who knows the secrets of Word, the one colleague proficient with databases, the other who has learned Java in her spare time, and the one who knows how to nurse the server all contribute."[13]

## Learning from the Past: Jazz and John Dewey

At first consideration, the idea of jamming and hanging out as a kind of ultimate education has, I suspect, a strongly bohemian feel to it: nightclubs and late-night coffeehouses scattered around Manhattan and north in Harlem. And indeed New York City was the setting for many important and famous jam sessions. In the 1940s, well-known musicians such Ben Webster and Lester Young would regularly show up at a club called Minton's Playhouse. The legendary Thelonious

Monk was the house pianist; Charlie Parker and Dizzy Gillespie would come to play after hours. Younger musicians came to watch and hear and wait their own turns on the bandstand, while musicians held "cutting sessions," trying to outdo each other by playing extremely fast or extremely complex chord changes. Bebop was invented here. There were also famous "cutting contests" in which musicians would trade segments back and forth to see who could keep up. The stride pianists James P. Johnson and Willy "The Lion" Smith used to engage in these "battles" after hours in Harlem homes. Whenever Art Tatum showed up, he would win.

Yet frantic and outré as it often could be, this kind of *learning through active doing*, through leaping in and initiating a course of action, spinning accounts of fragmented worlds, getting responses and ideas from others, and trying again and again, has an impeccable academic pedigree. The great early twentieth-century education reformer John Dewey saw clearly that learning is far more about social process than we tend to believe. Hence, the title of his most famous work, *Democracy and Education*, in which he argued that schooling was about more than knowledge accretion; it was about learning how to live.

First, Dewey did not like the traditional approach of measuring intelligence as if it were a capacity locked within each person's skull. He believed we are all natural learners, potentially curious and eager to explore fresh alternatives and responses, given the appropriate supportive setting. This natural learning is interrupted by traditional teaching methods that involve explicit assertions and rote memorization. Traditional teaching, he feared, can kill natural curiosity.

Dewey imagined learning as a process that disrupts routines on the way to making connections between unfamiliar experiences and familiar contexts. Learning and thinking involve *active inquiry*, a search for "something not quite at hand"—exploration, that is, beyond the realm of the familiar and conventional, of habitual practice patterns. Learning, Dewey felt, involves risk taking because one can never predict the outcome of the consequences of experimental activity. I've been a schoolboy, a doctoral student, a jazz pianist, and for twenty-two years a professor of management. I can write with absolute certainty that no single activity better fulfills Dewey's multiple dicta than what I have been writing about in this chapter: jamming, hanging out, those learning and practicing communities that spring up spontaneously when we acknowledge that education is, in fact, about more than knowledge. It's about learning how to live.

There are some important insights here. When you're learning to be a professional, it's not just a matter of memorizing a set of rules or a stock of explicit knowledge. Often what you are learning is an outlook, a mood, a disposition. You're learning to absorb a whole way of being—picking up practices, rather than learning about practices. This learning is anything but clean, rote, or logically arranged. Learning to be a practicing musician, like learning to be a practicing executive, is a sloppy process. It's intuitive and vague. You are guessing and adjusting, trying to grasp what to do next, listening to how others grapple with dilemmas, imitating the phrases and facial expressions of admired peers, trying something based on vague glimpses and threads of meaning—and, critically, reorienting as you go.

This kind of learning involves trying, getting stuck, and then trying again. With jazz players, as with rising executives and junior partners, this is a work in progress that's performed in public. But the presence of others and the stories they share make a difference. Just as a division head in a meeting learns the proper way to critique an idea and how to receive and give critiques in public settings, the jazz musician learns the norms of meta-learning, how to help others think, how and when to give advice—crucial skills for everyone.

## Relationships, Not Individuals

Important, paradigm-changing innovations are typically associated with individual creativity and genius. In the fourteenth century,

Johannes Gutenberg invented the printing press. In the eighteenth century, James Watt invented the steam engine, and Eli Whitney, the cotton gin. During the nineteenth century, Thomas Fulton figured out the steamship; Samuel F. B. Morse, the telegraph; Alexander Graham Bell, the telephone; and Gugliemo Marconi, the radio. In the last century, Henry Ford created innovations for the assembly line and produced the modern automobile; Bill Gates and Paul Allen—but mostly Gates in popular lore—came up with a practical computer user system; and Steve Jobs seemingly invented just about everything else that's popular today.

The list goes on and on, but no one holds a more prominent spot on it than Thomas Edison, the Wizard of Menlo Park, the inventor of the light bulb, the phonograph, and so much more. Only a genera-tion or two ago, schoolchildren were commonly taught that Edison was so dedicated to invention and so driven by the swirl of ideas in his head that he commonly slept in his rolltop desk rather than risk being away from his lab when inspiration struck. The *New York Times* caught all this dramatically in its October 18, 1931, obituary for one of America's most famous sons:

> *No figure so completely satisfied the popular conception of what an inventor should be. Here was a solitary genius revolutionizing the world and making an invisible force do his bidding—a genius that conquered conservatism, garlanded cities in light, and created wonders that transcended the predictions of utopian poets.*[14]

Yet as Andrew Hargadon points out, this glorification of individual genius is thoroughly misleading. What gets overlooked are the *interactions through which innovations develop*. When we ask questions about where ideas come from, as in the study of Edison and the "invention" of the light bulb, the story is far more complex than the popular conception.

Designing opportunities for serendipity is another way of saying yes to the mess. It's a way of acknowledging that we cannot control when and how learning will occur; we cannot be sure what the most important idea or insight is to move forward. But the *yes* is an affirmative leap, a willingness to move forward with no guarantee of what's going to emerge, how others will respond, or where you're going to end up. Celebrating serendipity means that you can blunder into an unfolding possibility that can come out of the periphery of the familiar. Often the most significant, accidental, surprise moments of discovery occur in informal, unplanned settings.

Edison, in fact, understood very well the learning potential of informally hanging out with a collection of diverse specialists. In a sense, Edison was holding jam sessions that led to his own version of bebop. He assembled a group at Menlo Park—ten to fifteen engineers from different industries and backgrounds. They essentially played together, intimately experimenting and learning together as they tried out wild ideas. The groups led by Edison learned from telegraph signals, generators, and a variety of other industries and specialties. Hargadon puts it bluntly: "Edison neither invented the light bulb nor acted alone in improving upon it. The web around Edison was thick with ties to other people, ideas, and objects that together made up his particular invention."[15]

In his biography of Steve Jobs, Walter Isaacson tells the story of Jobs's design of a building that would maximize hanging out and serendipitous conversations. Pixar had been a fledgling animated movie studio. But after *Toy Story 2* was a big hit, Jobs and the directors at Pixar decided it was time to build a new building. Director John Lasseter was imagining a traditional Hollywood studio with separate buildings for the different functions and projects. But Jobs felt that such a structure would create too much isolation and opted for a design that almost forced informal interaction. Jobs insisted on "one huge building around a central atrium designed to encourage random encounters."[16] Isaacson writes that Jobs felt the digital world can be too isolating:

> *Jobs was a strong believer in face-to-face meetings. "There's a temptation in our networked age to think that ideas can be developed by email*

*and iChat," he said. "That's crazy. Creativity comes from spontaneous*
*meetings, from random discussions. You run into someone, you ask what*
*they're doing, you say 'Wow,' and soon you're cooking up all sorts of*
*ideas."*[17]

Thinking like a jazz musician who had learned how important it is
to hang out and jam, Jobs insisted that the building be designed to
encourage spontaneous conversations and improvised collaborations.
"If a building doesn't encourage that, you'll lose a lot of innovation
and the magic that's sparked by serendipity," he said. "So we designed
the building to make people get out of their offices and mingle in the
central atrium with people they might not otherwise see." All rooms
are connected to the atrium. In fact, the original design called for
only one set of bathrooms to be connected to the atrium. Lasseter
said "Steve's theory worked from day one. I kept running into people
I hadn't seen for months. I've never seen a building that promoted
collaboration and creativity as well as this one."[18]

## Building In and On Diversity

Jazz players don't innovate by isolating or breaking off from others.
They don't wait for inspiration. They don't think of themselves as
creating something out of nothing. They innovate by being tightly
coupled to a diverse group of specialists, noticing the potential in people, ideas, and utterances. In a sense, they are engaged in constructive
arguments. They make comparisons with other people and different
activities, see the best in what already exists, and combine disparate
parts in new ways. Jazz musicians do what Edison did. They exploit
and connect various units and notice positive variations and redistrib-
ute emerging ideas.

The focus on individualism in invention has led to some popular aphorisms that now seem virtually unchallengeable. Managers

are encouraged to "think outside the box" and "push the envelope." Often to accomplish these ends, creative people and creative activity are isolated from the flow of organizational life. Thus, R&D groups are separated from the organization—physically as well as culturally. "Skunk Works" groups are created to break away from the ordinary culture so as to free the imagination to create a "game changer." As jazz shows us, though, creativity and innovation are inherently social accomplishments and involve linking with current and past activities, not separating from them. Experienced people need to have a chance to query one another, tell stories, and share wisdom. Separating creative types from day-to-day activity creates clean lines between "them" and "us," but it also can very quickly lead an organization to lose sight of and touch with disparate ideas and diverse specialists.

Consider, for example, the experiment that law professor Cass Sunstein conducted in two Colorado cities—one widely known to be politically conservative, Colorado Springs, and the other considered a politically liberal enclave, Boulder.[19] In each group, Sunstein first tested to see if there were any "outliers," so that if someone in Colorado Springs held a considerably more liberal view than the norm, he dismissed him or her from the experiment. He then put participants in small groups of five or six members and asked them to discuss controversial topics, such as global warming, same-sex marriage, and affirmative action— highly charged issues in American politics. People anonymously offered their opinions before and after the discussion groups.

What the experiment showed was at once both predictable and alarming. In almost all the groups, people held more extreme opinions after the discussions than they had before they began. In other words, hanging out in homogenous groups not only reinforced existing views but pushed people to more extreme opinions. And this was equally true on the conservative and liberal sides of the political spectrum. With both groups, mild diversities of opinion at the opening of the discussions disappeared as a consensus formed and gray areas shifted to black and white, evil and good.

Much the same thing happens regularly on the Internet and in ever-more segmented media groupings. Whether it's Facebook communities, blogs, or sports talk shows, invisible borders quickly form that drive out diversity, flatten opinion, and raise the heat. Discussion becomes shouting. Moderate becomes extreme until it's our way or the highway. What are the chances of being surprised in any of these venues? Of making a new discovery? In truth, there's almost none. Be careful how you design the hanging-out sessions so that your prior leanings and prejudgments don't just get affirmed and reinforced.

That's not what jazz is. Jazz involves jamming with people who don't see things exactly the same way. Jazz is about creating a venue where experimentation is the norm, where people think out loud in all sorts of directions and articulate their half-formed thoughts without feeling they have to be perfect or right or defensive or conform to any orthodoxy before offering an insight. Great jazz leaders like Miles Davis, Duke Ellington, and Art Blakey knew this. They consciously maximized diversity in order to guard against too much consensus. Trumpeter Sean Jones says that for Davis, a unique personality could count just as much as talent:

> Miles hired such different musicians because he was always looking for a sound that was never created before . . . If you hire your own friends, it becomes a clique. If you hire people from everywhere, you can create your own vibe immediately. No one has inhibitions because no one is coming from the same background. Miles Davis was very good at that, when he hired a band he never hired his friends. Sometimes he hired his enemies.[20]

Pianist Neil Cowley said something very similar: "If you stick with the same people, you tend to end up living in small towns drinking in the same pub and not developing as a person, and then you become a bit reactionary and then you need to start worrying that you are starting to die from within."[21]

For musicians as for human resources directors, diversity isn't always the easy route. Miles Davis's bands had plenty of conflict. For one album session, he actually invited two extraordinarily accomplished pianists to be on hand: Wynton Kelly *and* Bill Evans. Kelly performed regularly with Davis and was angry and confused that Davis had asked another pianist to join them. In fact, Evans plays in every song on that album except for the one in which Kelly performs. But this was a case where the end surely justified the means. The name of that album was *Kind of Blue*, one of the greatest jazz recordings of all time.

## Hanging Out Across Boundaries: Crowdsourcing as Cyber-Jamming

In the previous chapter, we looked at various examples of Wikipedia and Linux forms of crowdsourcing as examples of the interplay between minimal structure and guided autonomy. Wikipedia, for example, has become a globally accessible and almost inexhaustible resource based on a very few rules inviting autonomous contributions that are, considered in the aggregate, astoundingly accurate. (The error rates for Wikipedia are only slightly higher than those found in *Encyclopedia Britannica*.) Here we look at the same phenomena from a different angle because, as with jamming, the crowdsourcing movement is equally about the crowd itself.

One thing the postmodern world has made abundantly clear is that important knowledge resides outside the boundaries of singular groups and even outside the boundaries of any one organization. To become and remain innovative, organizations need to find ways to connect to these networks and promote learning across traditional borders. Centralized models of planning and control simply won't work when there are so many smart people distributed across so many sectors. The open-source movement and crowdsourcing take all that as a given and go on to assume that closed and proprietary models of innovation are therefore no longer viable agents of change. In important ways, open sourcing is an attempt to foster serendipity. As with jamming, these are standing invitations to multiple voices to contribute specialized perspectives.

Consider again the Linux operating system. Linux has grown from ten thousand lines of code to over four million lines because of the voluntary contributions of thousands of participants.[22] The collaboration is loose and informal. As is so often the case with jazz musicians, the initial "jamming" invitation from Linus Torvalds, the "founder" of Linux, was marked by fun and user need.

> *Hello netlanders,*
>
> *Do you pine for the nice days of the minix-1.1, when men were men and wrote their own device drivers? Are you without a nice project and just dying to cut your teeth on an OS you can try to modify for your own needs? . . .☺*
>
> *I'm doing a (free) operating system, just a hobby, won't be big and professional . . .*
>
> *I'd like any feedback on things people like / dislike . . . This is a program for hackers by a hacker. I've enjoyed doing it, and somebody might enjoy looking at it and even modifying it for their own needs . . . Drop me a line if you are willing to let me use your code.*
>
> *Linus (torvalds@kruuna.helsinki.fi)*[23]

Users were invited to download and modify the source code to suit their needs and interest and to do so out of sheer intrinsic pleasure—in other words, for the fun of learning. Torvalds asked that the modified source codes be sent back to him so that he could then share with the wider community. Soon a communitywide Internet forum took hold and the community virtually exploded. People now use these forums to help each other solve technical problems and consider novel applications. According to Karim Lakhani and Jill Panetta, the founding values haven't changed.

*Although over the past 16 years the number of people and firms inter-*
*ested in Linux has continued to grow, the basic model of participation*
*on the basis of user need or curiosity and having fun has not changed.*
*To participate one need only sign up for the Linux kernel mailing*
*list (LKML) and be competent to modify source code . . . participants*
*report and fix bugs, contribute and modify code, and discuss the tech-*
*nical evolution of the kernel . . . much of the development is organic,*
*determined by the actions of community members and not by any*
*measure of explicit project management within the community.*[24]

The loose and informal collaboration that got started here is essentially what jazz musicians do. Out of sheer enjoyment of learning and
mutual curiosity, they share ideas across boundaries, and a community
grows up organically around the experience. None of this is organized
by specific project management or any form of preplanned control.
Indeed, it would seem that a responsible manager would not want
to allow complex technology to develop in such random, distributed
ways. But the key thing is that it works.

Companies such as TopCoder have realized that they can design,
develop, and maintain software systems by drawing upon a virtual
community of volunteers. TopCoder has a global community of over
225,000 developers who write software modules for its clients, and
none of them are employees or "owned" by the company. The company sets up online competitions in which volunteer developers work
to design and propose software modules.

As with Linux, these TopCoder communities have much in common with jazz musicians. Everyone is learning by hanging out. It's a
distributed innovation system in which problem solving is decentralized, participants freely choose to join the conversation, and they self-
organize and coordinate among themselves.

Even the Department of Defense has discovered crowdsourcing and shown to its satisfaction that it works. In December 2009,
the Defense Advanced Research Project Agency, the innovative arm

of the Pentagon better known as DARPA, tested the concept with something it called the Network Challenge. DARPA challenged teams formed via social networking to find ten balloons hidden across the United States in undisclosed locations. A group of 5,400 people from MIT found all the balloons within nine hours. Convinced that there is wisdom in crowds and untapped value in simply hanging out, DARPA has repeatedly gone to the wider community to solicit ideas about technology, ranging from spacecraft software to military vehicles.[25]

## Gathering Around Sound

One of the most inventive of the open-source companies has been Threadless. In 2000, Threadless managers came up with the idea of soliciting T-shirt designs, posting them on its Web site, and then allowing members of the company's online community to vote on which designs they wanted turned into actual products. Not many years before, FedEx had had the genius idea of turning the traditional role of packing and shipping clerk over to its customers. Threadless went a quantum leap further by turning its R&D and marketing over to its customer base as well.

A more recent Threadless innovation has added social utility to the mix. The online Threadless Atrium is, according to the Web site, "a place to collaborate for one purpose: to turn great ideas into tangible products that matter and make a difference." The three-step process is basic to Threadless: the company and an ad hoc partner post a design challenge, the online community submits designs consistent with the challenge and picks favorites, and Threadless makes products from the best designs. But the "partners" in the Atrium competition are laudable causes: help for the victims of the New Zealand earthquakes, for example, or the earthquake–tsunami–nuclear disaster in Japan. The winners get (in addition to very modest, specific rewards) airtime on

"Threadless TV" to talk about their design and how it was inspired by the crisis at hand.

The Threadless slogan for its Atrium gets right to the point: "Gather Around Design." That's just what the company does—gathers and sustains a creative community around design, lets it jam and hang out together (at least in cyperspace), and trusts the process to generate a product that will have social utility.

How different is this from jazz? Hardly a lick. Jazz *is* crowdsourcing. Jazz shares. It trades. In the marketplace of what gets played and remembered, jazz also votes. We can argue all we want about the social utility of jazz—I happen to think it's high—but as an art form and mode of education, jazz is certainly learning by acting, by doing, by social exchange. With jazz, you master notes and chords, how to blow into a horn instrument and coax sound from strings or a drumhead or what have you. But you also learn how to be and do and live. You say yes to the mess by surrendering control—by opening yourself up to the capriciousness of the crowd, with no guarantee of success for your efforts. Ultimately, that takes one quality above all others: courage.

# CHAPTER SIX

# Taking Turns Soloing and Supporting

## Followership as a Noble Calling

"Lead, follow, or get out of the way"—that old adage pretty much sums up conventional wisdom about the corporate pyramid. At the top are the chief executives who give us direction. Next come the followers, who fall in line behind (unless they want to be part of the problem). At the base is everyone else—the ones who muddle around and obstruct the way. Little wonder that boards, investors, and other stakeholders become so fixated on identifying CEOs who can fill the role of fearless leader, however huge the raid he or she might entail on the corporate coffers.

Once, most CEOs rose through the ranks to take control of a company they knew intimately. Now, CEOs are just as likely to be chosen from outside, rather than promoted from within. If the company has a big enough global footprint, the CEO is also likely to achieve something like rock-star status. In 1980, exactly one CEO graced the cover of *Business Week*. By 2000, nineteen of the magazine's fifty-two covers featured CEOs.

Why the difference? In his wonderful book *Searching for a Corporate Savior: The Irrational Quest for Charismatic CEOs*, Rakesh Khurana argues that we have become more focused on the individual CEO as the creator of corporate wealth. It's the leader, not the business, that drives stock prices, or so the media would often have us believe. Indeed, when it was announced in the summer of 2011 that Steve Jobs would be taking a second medical leave from his post at Apple, newspapers and cable stations led their reporting with speculation on how far Apple's share price would fall on the news. (Answer: About $7 on day one, only to recover in fairly short order. But news of the recovery was miniscule compared to predictions of share-price Armageddon.)

Publishing houses help reinforce the media-driven cult of the business leader. In the aftermath of wars, memoirs by victorious generals flood the bookshelves. In times of prosperity, CEOs like Lee Iacocca and Jack Welch become best-selling philosopher-kings. Meg Whitman's tenure as CEO of eBay yielded both a top-selling memoir and a run for the U.S. Senate. In these lean times, many see Berkshire Hathaway's Warren Buffett as a rare voice of reason amid our hopelessly mired politics.

Scholars and analysts also help perpetuate this view of leaders as individual heroes, the animating force behind big causes, epic moves, earthshaking shifts, and tremors. Jim Collins's *Good to Great* deified the charismatic boss, while limning the underlying essence of a person or type that makes a great leader. Business schools further enshrine the cult of the leader by devoting entire institutes to the subject of leadership, and graduate business students, quite understandably, fall in line as well. After all, if you're not a leader, you're a follower, or worse. Who gets to the C-suite that way?

I brought up this issue a few years ago when I was teaching a class in the negotiation program to seventy-five MBAs at Harvard Business

School. Here's what I said: "I was looking through the course cata-
logue today, and I noticed how many elective courses are offered on
leadership at HBS. It's really remarkable, and I know these courses are
popular. In fact there's a waiting list to get in them. I've been thinking
about offering a course on followership. I'm curious. How many here
would be interested in taking a course on followership next semes-
ter?" Not a single person raised his or her hand. There were laughs and
chuckles throughout he class. The message was clear. No one wants to
be a follower.

Jazz teaches a different aesthetic. Jazz shows us that followership can
be not just satisfactory work but a noble calling. And it all begins with
the ear.

## Generous Listening

*The thing that sets Roy apart from other musicians is that he listens
so well. He teaches you to listen carefully and to respond accordingly, to
put things in perspective, not to simply go out for yourself.*
       —Pianist McCoy Tyner, describing drummer Roy Haynes[1]

*Group improvisation is a further challenge. Aside from the weighty
technical problem of collective coherent thinking, there is the very
human, even social need for sympathy from all members to bend for the
common result.*

                                                         —Bill Evans[2]

As we've seen, jazz thrives on improvisation; there's no clear road
map that tells people how to act in order to coordinate with one
another. The only route available to them, in fact, is listening. Jazz
musicians *have* to heed one another closely; they need to be attentive
not only to what each member is doing and saying but also to what
no one is doing or saying. When someone asked Miles Davis how he

improvises, he said that he listens to what everyone is playing and then plays what is missing.

So open, appreciative, and generous was Davis's ear that he could hear strengths even when weaknesses were shining through. When Davis first heard John Coltrane play, he might well have picked up on what so many others noticed: Trane's occasional awkwardness or the squeaks that would intermittently disrupt his lines. But that's not what caught Davis's attention. He heard Trane's creative impulse—his willingness to take risks, his unique voice, and unpredictable phrases. Davis heard what could be, not merely what was: a huge difference.

This is generous listening at its best, an unselfish openness to what the other is offering and a willingness to help others be as brilliant as possible. Being generous is not the same as simply being uncritical. In jazz as in any other endeavor, people get stuck in phrases and modes. Not everyone has to suffer until he or she finds a way through. But generous listening does mean being acutely aware of where the other is *heading*—of someone else's sense of future possibilities. There's a selfless suspension of ego in these moments when you make the other primary and seek to further his or her contributions. In essence, generous listening means you are willing to become the thinking partner of your immediate colleagues, helping them navigate through the terrain of obstacles they face while fashioning a way forward.

In jazz, generous listening expresses itself first and foremost in what is known as "comping": the rhythms, chords, and countermelodies with which the other players accompany a solo improvisation. ("Comp" is short for "accompany.") Not surprisingly, comping goes to the very soul of the art form.

Is it possible for members of an organization to do the same—to accompany others' thinking so that ideas achieve fruition, just as jazz players comp each other's playing to bring the music to its fullest expression? Yes, of course, but doing so requires letting go of automatic patterns. Organizational members have to make room for one another, suspend efforts to manipulate and control outcomes, relinquish investment in predetermined plans, and often surrender familiar protocols. To agree to comp, in other words, is to accept an invitation of openness and wonderment to what unfolds.

In an organization that stresses comping, ideas rise and fall based on their own merits rather than who originates them. The journey of discovery takes precedence over positional authority. In comp organizations, people are encouraged to think out loud, to have open conversations, knowing that others are listening and building on one another's sparks. The immediate goal is to help ideas and insights emerge, and to get there, everyone has to be especially sensitive to the initial steps, the moments when ideas are most fragile. The larger goal is to mobilize the intelligence and spirit of groups throughout the system.

None of this is easy to accomplish. Traditional hierarchies get subverted when organizations learn to comp. Patterns of deference have to be revamped. Hearing takes precedence over being heard. But when organizations are able to embrace the spirit of generosity that typifies jazz improvisation at its best, it is the equivalent of rediscovering fire.

## Taking Turns Leading and Following

There's a fundamental paradox to the cult of the leader. We in the business world spend enormous time and energy honoring and rewarding individual achievement—as does the business media—yet we know at a fundamental level that innovative breakthroughs are far more likely to result from social relationships, from conversations and dialogues between diverse groups with divergent skills, than they are from individual strokes of genius. Why don't we tell that story—about the others who were in the room when the great idea was first articulated and about the followers, not the leaders, who took a half-baked concept seriously enough to help it become palatable and marketable?

The reason, I suspect, is that followership is so devalued, yet the simple fact is that improvisation cannot succeed—whether the medium is jazz, comedy teams, or new product development—unless the players are extraordinarily adept at both leadership *and* followership. Indeed, the simple practice of taking turns leading and supporting might be the single practice *most* responsible for relational breakthroughs.

Here again jazz provides a ready model. Jazz bands routinely rotate the "leadership" of the band: that is, they *take turns soloing and supporting* other soloists by providing rhythmic and harmonic background. Each player has an opportunity to develop a musical idea, while others create space for this development to occur. In order to guarantee these patterns of mutuality and symmetry, players alternate comping one another.

In written arrangements, the scored passages often precede the soloist's improvisation and channel, sustain, and embellish it. In a sense, this background accompaniment conditions the soloist and organizes the course of the solo through passing chords, leading tones, and rhythmic accents. This, too, goes to the heart and soul of the art form: in every part of jazz, it is never enough to be an individual virtuoso; you must also be able to surrender virtuosity and enable others to excel.

In a supporting or comping role, musicians are interpreting the soloist's playing, anticipating likely future directions, and making instantaneous decisions regarding harmonic and rhythmic progressions. But they also may see beyond the player's current vision, perhaps provoking the soloist in a different direction, with accents and chord extensions. None of this responsiveness can happen unless players are receptive and taking in one another's gestures. But this empathy has to run in both directions. As a soloist, the same obligations prevail. You have to be listening just as generously as you are listened to and be just as receptive to fresh directions.

If everyone tries to be a star and does not engage in supporting the evolution of the soloist's ideas, the result is bad jazz. I've sat in on sessions like that. It's torture. If the soloist forgets about those who are comping him, the results are just as bad. It's the symbiosis that makes jazz work at its best—when players listen well forward and backward, from soloist to accompaniment and back again. Usually we think that great performances create attentive listeners. This notion suggests a reversal: attentive listening *enables* exceptional performance.

Here's how pianist Roland Hanna talked about his thirty years of collaboration with the bassist Richard Davis:

> *[I] have an idea of what he might play from one note to the next. If he plays a C at a certain strength, then I know he may be looking for an A flat or an E flat or whatever direction he may go in. And I know he may be making a certain kind of a passage. I've heard him enough to know how he makes his lines. So I may not know exactly what note he's going to play, but I know in general the kind of statement he would make, or how he would use his words, you know, the order he would put his words in . . . We train ourselves over a period of years to be able to hear rhythms and anticipate combinations of sounds before they actually happen.*[3]

Imagine how corporate life might be transformed by this kind of mutual reliance—a culture in which you know you're not in it alone; in which you know that others are thinking with you and about you, helping to make you even better—a culture in which, to paraphrase the jazz saxophonist Lee Konitz, you know that if you miscalculate or go down for a second, all you have to do is keep quiet and let someone else play for a moment, and the music will continue to grow.[4] Could there be a better model of social creativity—this calling to support others so that they might shine? It reminds me of a phrase from scripture: "He who humbles himself will be exalted."

## Opening Up the Silence

The best organizational learning involves accepting a *soloing and supporting* mind-set. To get there, leaders need to master the art of leading and followership, just as members of a jazz band do. The deceptively simple practice of taking turns creates a mutuality structure that guarantees participation, inclusion, shared ownership, and organizational dialogue, all of which can lead to dynamic capability in organizations, just as it does in jazz. Nurturing this dual mind-set also allows novel ideas to come from voices that may have been traditionally silenced.

IDEO has institutionalized this notion of support. When the company holds brainstorming sessions for new product ideas, there is a clear sense of competition between participants over who has more ideas or better ideas. But there is also a very explicit rule that's actually posted on the wall: "Don't criticize someone else's idea." In fact, participants are expected to build on others' ideas, to follow and comp, to assume that there is value in someone else's suggestion and to elaborate and build upon it. In such a culture, nascent ideas stay alive longer and people help one another become more articulate—even brilliant.

Recent research on collective intelligence shows that when people are listened to deeply, groups themselves become more articulate and brilliant. In their recent *Science* article, Anita Woolley et al. found that groups in which a few people dominated the conversation were less collectively intelligent than other groups in which there was a more equal distribution of turn taking in conversations.[5] Other studies of distributed leadership in schools and collaborative intelligence provide further support for the powerful value of simply taking turns. As Richard Hackman notes, "Team leadership is not a solo activity . . . shared leadership is an extraordinarily valuable resource for accomplishing the full array of leadership functions needed for team effectiveness."[6]

This is more than simply "job rotation." Taking turns soloing and supporting is ultimately about taking turns at egocentric passion and other-centric compassion. The first of those, egocentric passion, is endemic to corporate settings and probably a necessary evil as well. Enterprises need people to drive them forward. But many of the constituents of egocentric passion—excessive competition for stardom, a need to be in unilateral control, efforts to defend one's position against challenges, hesitancy to acknowledge the limits of one's knowledge—are clear obstacles to the learning process.[7]

Other-centric compassion is far rarer in the corporate setting, but arguably of greater value. Organizational innovation thrives when all members are given room to develop themes, to think out loud and discover as they invent. Given the complex and systemic nature of problems that cross conventional boundaries, managers—as knowledge specialists—cannot be solo operators: They *need* one another's expertise and support in order to arrive at novel solutions.

For a model of what an organizational jam session might look like, consider the "ValuesJam" that Sam Palmisano instituted in 2003, soon after becoming CEO of IBM—a seventy-two-hour Web chat about what the company stands for, open to over 350,000 IBMers in 270 countries. One board member questioned whether this was "socialism," but Palmisano nonetheless proceeded, with considerable success.[8] Approximately 140,000 IBMers participated, and IBM even found itself a new values statement as a result.

Liam Cleaver, director of IBM's Jam program office, describes the ValuesJam as "a watershed event" for the company. "I think it truly redefined the relationship between employees and management [by] tapping into the natural creativity and passion that people have about wanting to make the place they work better."[9]

Emboldened by success, the company was back at it again three years later, with its first Innovation Jam, an online brainstorming session that brought together 150,000 people from 104 countries and launched 10 new businesses under the IBM umbrella. That jam was repeated again in 2008 with equal success.

These online collaborative discussions, in Cleaver's words, "serve as a spark, really a catalyst for change within an organization." But they are open-ended and not driven by an "I'm okay, you're okay" mind-set. This is worth repeating: good comping is not the same as agreement. Whether it's a jazz jam or an innovation one, helping people to be at their best sometimes means challenging them to get on track, waking them up, and feeding them ideas that will help get them unstuck. The jams, Cleaver says, are "a way to really harness the creativity and innovation of a group of people on . . . a specific set of topics. So it's not a free-for-all, but it's a very focused conversation for a practical outcome."[10]

These are practices—and opportunities—that go way beyond business. In 2005, IBM partnered with the Canadian government and a United Nations agency to host Habitat Jam, a global discussion on urban sustainability. More recently, the company has begun to market the concept through www.collaborationjam.com.

What would happen if this idea of taking turns soloing and supporting were to become more widespread in organizations—if employees, managers, and executives were evaluated on their capacity to surrender self and ego in an effort to support the development of another's idea; if companies began recognizing and rewarding in significant ways those who strive to nourish, strengthen, and enhance the expressive capacity of relationships; if companies were to expressly value synchronistic, supportive leadership?

It's not as easy as it might sound. Jams, directed crowdsourcing, whatever you want to call them, are inherently a time of uncertainty because there can be no guarantee if any appropriate ideas will emerge. Supporting this sort of collaborative leadership-followership means having the courage to take initial steps in new situations, when people want principles of certainty, but where no rules are appropriate. It's a leap, in short, but IBM's experience suggests that such enterprises would unleash their capacity to improvise and innovate. The history and practice of jazz tells us the same thing.

# Why Some Groups Are Smarter Than Others

I wrote earlier that collective intelligence makes groups smarter, but not all groups are created equal. Researchers at MIT investigating the dynamics of collective intelligence have discovered multiple factors that make some groups smarter than others. In particular, three factors differentiated the high-performing, smart groups from their lower-performing peers.

- The first factor is what the researchers call social sensitivity. These groups were high in empathy, able to read one another's emotions. The capacity to tune into what others were thinking, feeling, and sensing helped the intellectual capacity of the entire group. In the following chapter, we'll look in detail at Miles Davis's seminal jazz album *Kind of Blue*. For now, let me cite a single moment when Davis is soloing and the pianist Bill Evans is so attuned to him that he plays the exact same phrase along with Davis. The term *empathy* is almost not strong enough to capture this dynamic of deep attunement.

- The second factor that differentiates smart groups is inclusive involvement and turn taking, just as in jazz bands. Groups in which leaders took more airtime, talked a great deal, and left less room for others performed poorly. We've all been in these situations, and for the most part we have learned to simply tolerate the long-windedness, but what we forget is that the collective intelligence of the entire system is suffering. (Jack Welch once said that it takes a lot of self-confidence *not* to say everything that you know.) This is where comping becomes more than simply passive listening. If the soloist is repeating routines, the person comping might give him a slight kick to encourage him to stop trotting out the old familiar phrases and opinions. Ken Peplowski once did that to me when he heard me playing a lick that had grown overly familiar. He started repeating it to get me off the dime and start thinking in fresh ways. People sometimes need others to disrupt their routines and clichés.

- The third factor that the researchers found is provocative but in a sense almost predictable from the first two. Groups with a higher proportion of females outperformed groups made up of mostly males. Why? The researchers hypothesized that this points back to the earlier factor regarding sensitivity: women are better socialized in sensitivity and making room for others. Whatever the actual reason, the collective lesson of the MIT research is clear: organizations can up their IQ by striving to make everyone sensitive to the intelligence of the collective and the dynamics that make groups smarter.[11] Why be dumb when you don't have to be?

## Active, Not Passive Followership

There's a temptation to see supportive roles as a passive activity, an unfortunate connotation associated with the word *followership*. Followers are sheep, lemmings, and the ones who fall in line behind the alpha wolves, the CEO icons, or sometimes the demagogues. The jazz prototype, though, tell us that this is far from the truth. Generous listening through comping is a very active, committed, and even risky endeavor. When members are practicing this sort of followership, they are both standing their own ground and creating space: giving others room to experiment and supporting the unfolding of their ideas.

As we've seen, this is what jazz players do when they comp: they create a space that welcomes and acknowledges another person's current state of mind while also providing provocation that might rouse him or her to consider new possibilities. Here, too, there's a paradox at play: jazz players are expected to perform three seemingly mutually exclusive tasks—confirm, challenge or provoke, and continue—but comping works best precisely by making that connection, by doing all that at the same time.

In a way, comping behavior is what you might expect from a good friend—accept the other's ideas, pay attention to when the other might be stuck in an old pattern or routine that needs to be tweaked, imagine the other's positive potential, and help him or her be more articulate about things just out of reach. Good parenting calls for much the same skill set—the capacity to create what psychoanalyst Donald Winnicott has called a "holding environment" that supports children's cognitive development.[12]

Harvard psychologist and professor of education, Robert Kegan, took this notion of the holding environment and extended it to adult development. As adult learners, we too are dependent on a facilitating environment that provides understanding, empathy, and enough stability and freedom so that the "held" person feels enough safety and trust to branch out. A healthy group creates a good holding environment for all members, a space in which they can experiment with the awareness that they will receive empathy, understanding, support, and also challenge. In such holding environments, adults are better able to advance in learning and development. This holding environment is what jazz musicians supply for one another when they comp. Comping and a holding environment are both forms of what I call noble followership.

In Kegan's formulation, a holding environment performs three simultaneous functions: holding on, letting go, and staying in place. First, the environment holds well by mirroring back, meeting the person's needs through recognition and confirmation. It supports, recognizes who the person is in the moment by acknowledging how he thinks and feels, and by joining *"the very way he understands and interprets* the world (emphasis added)."[13]

Second, the environment needs to let go, challenging learners to extend beyond their current state and to reframe and rethink the way they are constructing the world. In this sense, the environment fights the comfort of affirmation and insists learners branch out to try something new and different, and follow their own intuition.

Third, a holding environment stays in place, maintaining a presence while the learner goes through the process of reframing and making sense of the novel situation, supporting the person who is becoming more than what he or she was, and helping the person to retrospectively make sense of what just happened.

This is just what musicians do when they take turns soloing and comping. They are creating a holding environment for one another.

## A Sense of Oneness

This notion of taking turns soloing and supporting is much easier to describe than to enact. Indeed, one of the problems with offering examples of good followership and support is that it is often invisible. We're not likely to notice someone who helps another be more articulate or see her idea through to fruition. Supportive followers by their very nature aren't inclined to brag about what a great job they did helping someone else flourish.

I was once writing a paper with my friend and colleague David Cooperrider. We had a tradition of spending one week each May at his family's cottage in Wisconsin working on papers. I wrote a section, and then he read what I wrote and picked up my language, extended it, and wrote four more pages and sent it back to me. I read what he wrote and noticed how he had affirmed it and taken it in an entirely different direction, suggesting possibilities I had never imagined. We went back and forth like this, and the final product eventually won a "best paper" award from the Academy of Management. Yet to this day, when I reread that paper, I cannot tell which sentences I wrote and which sentences Cooperrider wrote. Our prose soloing and comping became a single piece.[14]

Similarly, Hollywood writers who coscript sitcoms and other television episodes often report that they don't know who wrote which lines. Rather, as they sit together throwing out ideas, developing the story lines based on one another's inputs, and advancing a collective narrative, their separate voices blend into one.

There's also the example of Steve Nash, one of the National Basketball Association's all-time great point guards, widely known for his play-making and ball-handling skills. Nash's behind-the-back passes and full-court feeds have filled countless highlight reels. He makes things happen on a court when others can't even see the openings, much less take advantage of them. What's more, he's widely regarded as one of the smartest guards ever to play the game; in 2009, ESPN rated Nash the best passer and the player with the highest basketball IQ in the league. But it's not the fact that he "quarterbacks" but the *way* he quarterbacks a team that truly sets Nash apart.

Whether it's football or basketball, the stereotypical quarterback barks orders, takes command, and tells everyone on the court (or field) where to be when. Nash is different. He sees his on-court role far more in terms of helping others, noticing what kind of support they need so that they can thrive, and deliberately trying to complement their skills. Nash talked about this basketball equivalent of the holding environment in an interview with Charlie Rose:

> *I think the thing that people probably don't understand is that a point guard has to be a mother . . . has to be the psychologist, you know. It's not just strategic; it's psychological, too. And you have to understand, I think, not only the strategy and the tendencies of your teammates, but also their esteem at that moment, and you want their esteem to grow as the game and the season goes. And there's a lot to consider there, and there is a lot to notice and interpret. And I think to be a good point guard and to be a good teammate in general, you know, you need to be sensitive to those things as well . . . It's nonverbal—their shoulders, their eyes, the way they communicate nonverbally, it's so important to notice.*

Isn't it remarkable to hear a professional athlete talk about mothering his teammates? He went on:

> *I think that you try to care about your teammates. You try to have their best interest and the group's best interest simultaneously . . . It's in the best interest of the team to have everyone's best interest at heart, especially if you are feeding everyone . . .*
>
> *The final component for me is the feel . . . to know when to push, to know when to hold back, to know the nuances of the situation, whether it be psychology or strategy. The feel for the game is the one thing I think people underrate. And that is probably, you know, as important or more important—that feeling, that understanding the nuance.*[15]

That's a long quote, but it is also a wonderful, intuitive description of a holding environment and what it's like to take on the role of noble followership—supporting, understanding, and encouraging others so that they can shine. This is not only jazz and basketball at its best; it's a way for any organization to unlock its hidden potential.

## CHAPTER SEVEN

# Leadership as Provocative Competence

## Nurturing Double Vision

Duke Ellington was a widely acclaimed jazz composer, pianist, and big band leader, widely acknowledged as the most important composer in the history of jazz. He was brilliant at using the materials at his disposal to bring out the best in people, notice their unique voices, support their strengths, and create the conditions so that they could branch out and blossom. Ellington paid close attention to what players could do when they were at their best, how they played when they were doing well. He composed music specifically to match his players' strengths, their unique personalities, and their unique voice and sounds.[1]

Ellington looked for distinctive voices in his band and deliberately sought out diversity in sound. He was the first to introduce muted brass instruments combined with high clarinets. His harmonies were unique, often doubling instruments that no one else had considered

combining. Unlike most arrangers, he did not write parts anonymously for specific instruments, such as trumpets, trombones, and the
like. Instead, he wrote parts for the peculiar sounds and voices of people in his band, virtuosos such as Cat Anderson, Cootie Williams, and
Rex Stewart. Ellington was gifted at many things—composing foremost among them—but he was a master of relational coordination.

Mark Gridley wrote in his book *Jazz Styles*:

*Each one of Ellington's musicians had a highly individual sound.
So, even when they were not playing solos, their own unique way of
sounding each pitch was considered before giving them a particular part
to play. For example, if a chord was scored for three trumpets, Ellington
remembered the particular tone quality that each of his trumpeters ordi-
narily produced for each note in that chord, and he distributed the parts
of the chord to them to create the overall color he wanted that chord to
have in his arrangement. In addition, sometimes he would have one
trumpeter use a mute, another with no mute, and a third player sound
his note with an odd tone quality that only he was able to extract from
the trumpet. Ellington scored this way for saxes and trombones, too.
This is one reason that performances of Ellington's arrangements never
sound like Ellington's band when they are played by other musicians.*[2]

His trumpeter Cootie (Charles Melvin) Williams had a distinctive
style that involved using the mute plunger for unique shadings.
Williams could alter the size, shape, and quality of his sounds and
create a wide range of musical effects. He joined Ellington's band in
1929 and played with him for ten years. Several famous Ellington
recordings feature Williams, including "Concerto for Cootie," which
later became the hit song "Do Nothing Till You Hear from Me."
Never before had a trumpeter played with such a diverse style and
range, from mute to blaring high notes. Rather than forcing Williams
to conform to an "Ellington sound," Ellington created a vehicle for
Williams to branch out and discover his own voice.

Ellington had plenty of formal authority at his disposal, but he rarely used it when leading his band. There are legendary stories about dysfunctional conflicts between its members. Ellington seemed to treat it as an occupational hazard associated with creativity. When musicians were late to the bandstand, Ellington would simply start without them, sometimes picking tunes that were appropriate for a smaller ensemble. Moodiness, unreliability, and alcoholism were almost commonplace among his musicians. One player left the bandstand in the middle of a set to eat dinner. Yet with the exception of Charles Mingus, whose angry outburst at valve trombonist Juan Tizol had led Tizol to pull out his knife, Ellington never fired a member of his band, and even then, he reportedly told Mingus, "Charles, I don't fire musicians, so I must ask you to resign from my band."

Someone once asked Ellington why he put up with such rude and unpredictable behavior. His answer: "I live for the nights that this band is great. I don't think about the nights like what you're worrying about. If you pay attention to these people, they will drive you crazy. They're not going to drive me crazy."[3] Ellington's decision to focus attention on the band when they were playing brilliantly is a precious skill and central to provocative competence, as I will explain later.

## Fostering a Design Mind-Set

When it comes to leadership, we too often confuse authority with influence. We assume that what's important is to get enough authority so that you can have influence. *Yes to the Mess* proposes an alternative way of thinking about leadership activities: seeing them as relational moves within an unfolding context. In this model, leadership effectiveness is judged not by authority or how far up the pyramid people sit, but by how well they work with the resources at their disposal, no matter how limited, and how effectively they help free their own potential and that of others. As Karl Weick et al. wrote, "The order of organizational life comes just as much from the subtle, the small, the relational, the oral, the particular, and the momentary as it does from the conspicuous, the large, the substantive, the written, the general, and the sustained."[4]

In recent years, Richard Boland and his colleagues at the Weatherhead School of Management at Case Western Reserve University have been building on the work of Herbert Simon and looking at leadership through the lens of what's become known as the design mind-set.[5] Simon noticed that we often think of managers as decision makers, and in fact most MBA programs focus on techniques for good analysis and decision making. Perhaps, he posited, we should think of leaders and managers differently, not as making decisions based on past data, but as creating forms so that people can flourish in the future.

Instead of looking at leadership as decision making—as a rational process of sifting through data, analyzing trends, and making decisions based on predicting futures—a design framework emphasizes pragmatic experimentation. It sees managers as form givers, idea generators, agents who transform imperfect situations into better ones by questioning assumptions, exploring tangential ideas, and creating metaphors that stimulate thinking. Actions are experimental, and knowledge is applied, pragmatic, and ongoing rather than stable, objective, and predictive.

While a traditional, rational approach to understanding managerial action tends to favor analytic activities such as optimizing, minimizing risk, and selecting among predetermined activities, a design approach takes note of how managers shape worlds of interpretation in which others can make meaningful contributions. Leadership in this frame is a transformative process that calls for focusing on "third-order strategies" for carrying out second-order learning. In this context, leadership is much less about lines of authority or pyramidal hierarchies than it is about finding the far more subtle levers that influence productivity and performance. What and where are they?[6]

## Provocative Competence

Leadership as design activity means creating space, sufficient support, and challenge so that people will be tempted to grow on their own. The goal is the opposite of conformity: a leader's job is to create the discrepancy and dissonance that trigger people to move away from habitual positions and repetitive patterns. I've come to think of this key leadership capacity as "provocative competence."

The trombonist Milt Bernhart tells a story about Duke Ellington that beautifully illustrates his provocative competence. The band was to play a piece of music based on a movie. To get them started, Ellington put a single eight-bar line of music on each stand. "I looked down into those famous baggy eyes and asked, 'Pardon me, Duke. What'll we play besides the eight bars we've got?' His brows went up a fraction, and he said 'You'll know.' That was the end of the questioning period." This is a different art of leadership, designing just enough structure that constrains and guides the soloist to discover new possibilities.[7]

Trumpeter Clark Terry recalled another story that also illustrates Ellington's leadership style. One day, Ellington asked him to play like the trumpeter Buddy Bolden. "I said, 'Maestro, I don't know who the hell Buddy Bolden is!' Duke said, 'Oh sure, you know Buddy Bolden. Buddy Bolden was suave, handsome, and a debonair cat who the ladies loved. Aw, he was so fantastic! He was fabulous! He was always sought after. He had the biggest, fattest trumpet sound in town. He bent notes to the nth degree. He used to tune up in New Orleans and break glasses in Algiers! . . . As a matter of fact, you are Buddy Bolden!'"[8]

This, too, is provocative competence in action. First, it's clear that Ellington held an affirmative image of Clark Terry: he saw Terry at his best, appreciated his potential, and held on to that image even though Terry appeared confused and directionless. Notice all of the superlatives he used to describe Buddy Bolden—fabulous; fantastic; always sought after; biggest, fattest sound—and then how Ellington segued effortlessly into letting Terry know that he had been talking about him all along. Ultimately, Ellington gave Terry nothing more than a few suggestions, just enough to disrupt his routines and inspire him to stretch out. But Terry said that by the time they were done talking, he thought he was Buddy Bolden, ready to make the "biggest, fattest trumpet sound in town."

In jazz, as in business, we need leaders who do this—men and women who support imaginative leaps, who can create a context that enhances creative possibilities and triggers glimpses, sudden insights, bold speculation, imaginative ventures, and a willingness (even an insistence) that people explore new possibilities before there is certainty and before they fully comprehend the meaning of what they are doing. Leadership of this sort demands good design. These leaders have to create space that suggests possibilities, while also providing the right amount of constraints and limitations. They also need a capacity to notice peoples' potential, perhaps better than they see it themselves. Only then can leaders disrupt routines in a way that demands that people stretch themselves beyond their comfort level. This is what provocative competence is all about—leadership that enlivens activity and rouses the mind to life.

## Breaking Out of the Competency Trap

Research shows that successful organizations need to be careful. They have a tendency to fail to adapt, especially when faced with disruptive shocks and radical technological change and market shifts. As Clayton Christensen and others have demonstrated, it is often the very competence and patterns of success that have blinded these organizations and led to their downfall. Detroit's Big Three auto firms are a classic example. Decades of market dominance blinded Ford, GM, and Chrysler to the fact that the market itself had shifted dramatically. The very elements that success had rendered comfortable and automatic became traps that prevented meaningful change.

Other examples, of course, abound. The Walt Disney Company enjoyed enormous success with its U.S. theme parks, but when Disney attempted to extend that winning streak to Europe, executives were shocked by the mixed results. It turns out that the same systems and processes that worked in Florida and California didn't work in this context, with a totally different set of international players.

LEGO offers another example of the competency trap. Its core capability was in plastic toys. When electronic toys emerged in the 1990s, LEGO continued with its routine, doing what it did best and paying attention to traditional competitors while losing significant market share. Kodak likewise failed to address the implications of digital technology as a threat to its core business in paper and film, while Polaroid's senior managers couldn't recognize the need to compete in software rather than hardware. Back in the 1970s, Akron's many tire companies ignored the threat posed by radial tires. A decade earlier, Swiss watch manufacturers couldn't bring themselves to address quartz watch competition from Japan. Why bother, after all? Swiss watches were clearly better.

In many of these instances, the organizations had the innovative technology before their competitors did. Many also had foresight into the market changes and a sense of the environmental trends before their competitors, but they were simply unable to take advantage of their own ideas or bring their products to market. This is the nature of the competency trap—strengths and capabilities become rigidities that block learning and adaptation.

Jazz musicians face similar temptations every day—to favor exploitation of patterns, to rely on well-learned stock phrases and on licks that have been greeted enthusiastically in past performances, to become in effect imitations of themselves. To keep from falling into the competency trap, veteran players actively court what many might regard as risky, even perilous activity. They make deliberate efforts to create disruptions and incremental reorientations, hoping to outwit their learned habits by putting themselves in unfamiliar musical situations demanding novel responses, or they "trick" their automatic responses by throwing themselves into actual playing situations "over their heads," stretching themselves to play in challenging contexts.

"The search was always for something that sounded right to replace the things that sounded predictable and [therefore] wrong," Tony Oaxley once said.[9] Pianist Bill Evans continually practiced musical passages he did not quite understand, and once he mastered them, he took on other difficult passages.[10] Saxophonist John Coltrane deliberately played songs in difficult and unfamiliar keys because "it made [him] think" while he was playing, since he could no longer rely on his fingers to play the notes automatically. Keith Jarrett once put it: "You're never in a secure position. You're never at a point where you have it all sewn up. You have to choose to be secure like a stone, or insecure but able to flow."[11]

Herbie Hancock recalled how he was inspired to explore the unknown by hearing someone play a passage that he knew he couldn't duplicate. For some, this might be discouraging, but for Hancock, as for most successful jazz musicians, this was the beginning rather than the end of the story:

> I had been a musician all my life, had all this training, played with all these great players, but I knew I could never have created that. And if I can't do it, something is missing—I have to find out how to do it! I've always been like that when I've heard something I liked but I couldn't do. That's how I got into jazz. I heard this guy playing [jazz piano] at a variety show in high school, and I knew that he knew what he was doing, and he was doing it on my instrument—but I had no idea of what was going on. SO I wanted to learn how to do it. That's what got me started. In order to do that, you have to know what you don't know.[12]

Great jazz leaders work equally hard to keep their bands fresh. Hancock recalls that Miles Davis was very suspicious of musicians in his quartet playing repetitive patterns, so he forbade them to practice.

In an effort to spur the band to approach familiar tunes from a novel perspective, Davis would sometimes call tunes in different keys or call tunes that the band had not rehearsed. What's more, he would do this in concert, before a live audience. "I pay you to do your practicing on the bandstand," Hancock recalls Davis telling them. Such a high-risk strategy was dangerous enough with a seasoned band, but at the time Hancock is recounting, Davis's band was made up of mostly young players, in their early twenties. Drummer Tony Williams was in his teens, and the band had almost no experience playing together.

Keith Jarrett says that as part of Davis's commitment to "keeping the music fresh and moving," he steered away from his own pleasures as well. "Do you know why I don't play ballads any more?" Jarrett recalled Davis telling him. "Because I like to play ballads so much."[13]

## Cultivating Responsiveness and Dynamic Capability

Perhaps my favorite example of using provocative competence to beat the competency trap took place on March 2, 1959, at 2:30 in the afternoon in the Columbia recording studio. At the time, the jazz world was dominated by a style of music called bebop. Introduced by Dizzie Gillespie and Charlie Parker only a decade earlier, this music took the jazz world by storm and had become the measuring rod for jazz musicians. Bebop is hard-driving, fast music created by playing complicated patterns on top of intricate chords and syncopated phrases at an extremely fast tempo, often sounding like a flurry of notes. So nothing could have prepared the quintet for what Miles Davis introduced that day in 1959.

Davis had been hanging out with the jazz player George Russell, listening to and discussing innovative classical music, including Bartók, Stravinsky, and Schoenberg. Now, all the creative energy spawned by those get-togethers coalesced in rare fashion. When his unsuspecting quintet arrived in the studio, they were presented with sketches of songs—some only partially complete—written in unconventional modal forms using scales that were very foreign to western jazz musicians at that time.

One song, "So What," was minimally sketched without familiar chord changes, using two unusual modes, in a form the musicians had never played before. It's hard to appreciate how foreign this must have seemed. Yes, these were musicians used to innovation, but they also were accustomed to tackling songs in standard forms, playing notes that fit with the chords in some kind of familiar sequence, then repeating the form as each soloist took a turn playing on the changes. But for this song, "So What," there were no chords per se, at least ones that followed predictable patterns.

Davis was never one to give an excess of instructions, but this time he told his musicians simply to play on the scales. This was a whole new degree of freedom—there were no limits to what you played—but it also offered new restrictions: how do you know *what* to play? Musicians couldn't fall back on familiar habits that would help them feel competent as they traversed their way through unfamiliar territory.

Another song, "Blue in Green," contained ten bars instead of the more familiar eight- or twelve-bar form that characterized American popular music. Davis's quintet had never seen this music before, they were unfamiliar with the odd forms, *and* they had no rehearsal. The very first time they performed this music, the tape recorder was running. The result was the album *Kind of Blue*, widely regarded as a landmark jazz event—maybe *the* landmark event and the best-selling jazz recording in history.

*Kind of Blue* consists entirely of "first takes." When we listen to this album, we are witnessing the musicians approaching these pieces for the first time, simultaneously discovering new music and inventing it. Some have called it the perfect jazz album: melodic, lyrical, gripping, swinging, intellectually demanding, *and* completely spontaneous. Little wonder that the album should launch a musical revolution, changing not only the future of jazz, but also the future of rock and roll. Davis pushed the musicians to break the very rules and routines that underlay the way they knew and experienced the world of music.

Consider the first song recorded that day—the "So What" I just described. It began with Bill Evans playing a few chordal phrases in modal harmony and must have sounded slightly unusual to the musicians that day. Paul Chambers entered on bass with a two-bar phrase. Evans answered him with two chords that some have called an "amen" cadence because of the way it is phrased. I encourage you to listen to this historic piece because you can almost hear the musicians learning in real time. Davis took the first solo, and he began with three basic notes that seem to fall out of his horn. He repeated the three notes and returned to the phrase regularly as a kind of pivot that grounded him. As his solo developed, he departed from this phrase, and you become aware of the comping musicians in the background growing more confident in their playing.

There's even a famous error that occurred just as Davis's solo began. The drummer Jimmy Cobb kicked off the first solo with a cymbal crash, just as most drummers would do to introduce a hard-driving, bebop solo. The problem is that this is not a hard-driving bebop song. It has a laid-back, almost lazy feel. The cymbal crash sticks out like a sore thumb amid the quieter mood. Cobb said later that he knew it was a mistake immediately and assumed that they would have to retake the recording. But there was no second take that day, and this awkward cymbal crash can still be heard loudly and plainly.

When Davis finished his solo, it was John Coltrane's turn. Trane would later go on to master modal music, but on this date he was still learning, and the work was experimental even for him. What's interesting for our purposes is Trane's approach. He ran up and down the modal scale several times, as if to peruse the material at his disposal, like Picasso looking over his palette of colors as he began to paint. Here, too, you can hear the group becoming more confident as it supported Trane's solo. As in the story of the explorers wandering around the Swiss Alps with a map of the Pyrenees Mountains, this group wandered its way through the challenge that Davis set out. They took a few steps, repeated a prior phrase, ventured out, extended, and moved forward. And the effect is amazing: a group learning in real time as it created a historic piece of art.

Evans wrote two of the tunes, even though his authorship was not credited at first. For the song "Flamenco Sketches," Evans suggested five scales that expressed different moods, a very unusual way to construct a song. He wrote these words on the top of the music: "Play in the sound of these scales." This is about as vague a guideline as anyone is likely to find. What's more, he gave no direction about how long to play, how or when to move from one scale to the next, and what explicit chords to reach for. Instead, Evans played tone clusters and chromatic colors in the style of Ravel or Debussy. And the result is a classic piece of music in which the players stretch once again into heretofore unknown territory.

Three of the members from that band became leaders of their own bands, and each developed in remarkably different ways. Evans forever changed the style of the piano trio. Cannonball Adderly formed a group that played blues and bebop. Two years later, Davis formed the strongest and most influential quintet of his career, including Herbie Hancock, Tony Williams, Ron Carter, Wayne Shorter—and each of these went on to become a leader in his own right.

For his part, Coltrane became one of the world's premier jazz soloists over the next decade, but the influence of that single recording session would never leave him. He was already famous for piling chords on top of chords and playing them with such a degree of intensity that one critic had referred to his music as "sheets of sound," a label that stayed with him. On May 2, 1959, though, sheets of sounds were not enough. Fred Kaplan writes, "Yet rather than disorient him, as might have been expected, this session's shift from chords to scales sent Coltrane on a new, more sweeping trajectory. He still unfurled his sheets of sound, but since he no longer had to meet what [jazz theorist

George Russell] called 'the deadline of a particular chord,' he could vary his pace, focus more on rhythm, mood, and melody; his solos, while as virtuosic as ever, were more lyrical and lithe."[14]

In the next section, we will break down provocative competence into its component parts. For now, notice that Davis did not act on consensus. Much of the leadership literature suggests that leaders seek consensus from the group and get buy-in for their vision. However, like Ellington, Davis didn't ask for input before initiating these moves. If he had polled the quintet in advance and asked them how they felt about playing for a recording session in strange modes and forms, he would have gotten puzzlement, certainly, but not approval or consensus.

Also notice that neither Ellington nor Davis became overly attached to their own ideas. As a design activity, Davis put out ideas to see where they could go, but he guarded against falling too much in love with his own creations. Davis sent out probes and tentative prompts, but they were there mostly to spark conversation, to get activity going, something to play with. Leaders like this know that they don't create great things alone. They concoct directions to get groups moving, and they don't expect that all of them will work out. If a better idea emerges as a result, then it's not a failure, but there's no way of knowing initially. It's a state of continuous, reflexive inquiry.

## Deconstructing Provocative Competence

Provocative competence is, first, an *affirmative move*. What makes these interventions powerful is that the leader holds a positive image of what others are capable of. This often means seeing other people's strengths better than they see their own strengths. Davis knew that Coltrane, Adderly, and others had the capacity to play in these unfamiliar and perhaps uncomfortable modes and that they would make useful and even creative contributions. Just as important, he played to their strengths, not their weaknesses.

If a leader attempts provocation when focusing on a person's deficits or shortcomings, the gesture is likely to seem judgmental and punishing. Leaders who exhibit provocative competence are aware that this is a moment of *learning vulnerability*. Things could go either way. There's no guarantee that the experience will be successful, and in fact the players in the *Kind of Blue* session had no idea that they had made musical history until several years later when people began responding to the music and exploring its possibilities. These are moments of disquiet when people are momentarily off balance, and too much provocation or a provocation that calls attention to weaknesses is potentially fatal if you are trying to trigger discovery, receptivity, and openness. It's important to create a holding culture, an environment that provides enough stability and reassurance so that people know there is a safety net, someone to watch their backs as they branch out.

Second, provocative competence involves introducing a *small disruption to routine*. What makes provocative competence an "art" is the introduction of just enough unusual material that it engages people to be mindful—to pay attention in new ways. The disruption must be scaled appropriately. To that end, timing is critical. Leaders who disrupt on a regular basis or try to be provocative all the time are obnoxious, and are eventually ignored and probably mimicked. Too much disruption in the moment is also something to be mindful of. This is what makes provocative competence an art. In Davis's case, the disruption was scaled with a master's hand and a clear nod toward the affirmation just mentioned. Davis didn't suggest that the drummer play the piano, or the bass player, the sax. Those would have been little more than galling stunts. Rather, he disrupted routine just enough to free his quintet to go where it had never gone before.

Another element critical to provocative competence and well illustrated by the *Kind of Blue* recording session: it's key to create situations that *demand activity*. But further, it was not an "all or nothing" action. Players are expected to try and try again, to keep trying and discovering as they go. Passivity was not an option that day. The musicians couldn't step back, ponder awhile, and wait for someone else to do something. Once Davis counted off the song and started it, there was no turning back. People needed to leap in and start doing.

The fourth element in this process is *facilitating incremental reorientation by encouraging repetition*. The repetition constitutes, in effect, a comfort zone, but not one that is too comfortable. Even while people are leaning on old habits, they have to attend to new cues and new options, and start to manage and process information within a new, broader context. These are moments of gradual insight and slowly evaporating safety. As one of my jazz friends said to me, "Not all repetition is the same." Sometimes you need to repeat a gesture and then start to notice it from a slightly different angle. Hearing the traces of your gestures buoys you as you see fresh openings and explore other directions.

In *Kind of Blue*, you find this repeatedly in each of the players' solos. As noted earlier, Davis's first solo started with three simple notes. He repeated those notes in a slightly different pattern, but soon the notes sound quite different because they belong in a contextual framework that was simultaneously being created and discovered. This is another facet of the art of provocative competence: *leaders can't stop to judge too soon*. They need to encourage people to keep trying, to explore gestures and utterances for a potential appeal that might not become clear until much later.

The final element in our deconstruction of provocative competence is *analogic sharpening* of perspectives and thought processes. This is the point at which people look back at what is emerging and jump into the morass as they make comparisons, links, and connections to a larger, emerging whole. They link the familiar with new utterances, adjusting to the unanticipated in a way that reframes previous material. These are delicate moments in which each interpretation has implications for how one might proceed. People start to notice affinity between pieces that previously seemed disconnected; resemblances that no one noticed before start to emerge. Witness the way Cannonball Adderly soloed in *Kind of Blue*, making connections with the blues and bebop phrases he had played in the past. No prior planning would have made these linkages. Rather, under the guidance of provocative competence, people start to make parallel links with seemingly unrelated contexts and see linkages between seemingly disparate ideas.

On multiple occasions when I've spoken about provocative competence before business groups, the reaction, while broadly positive, has included a comment along these lines: "It's easy for you to use Miles Davis as an example. Look at the talented people around him. No wonder they created a great, historic album—they were wonderful instrumentalists. But what do you do when you have a less talented group or an underperforming team?"

The question is understandable, maybe even inevitable, but it misses the point in critical ways. Of course, different groups have different levels of performance, and leaders certainly have to deal with imperfect talent, but saying yes to the mess means *finding affirmation in the best of what already exists.* Every group, every individual has some strength, some moment of exceptional performance that has the potential to make a difference at some point. Truly gifted leaders—those who practice and exhibit provocative competence—are able to uncover this potential even when it is well hidden, even when the individuals in question can't see it in themselves. That's a true gift: to be able to see people at their very best when their current behavior is far less than that.

## Nurturing Double Vision

Socrates once said that wisdom begins with wonder. Is it possible for business leaders to create conditions that nurture wonderment?

I would argue that it's not only possible but obligatory. We have to recognize first, though, that this is a different mode of leadership. The literature on charismatic leadership insists on the need to create a clear vision and stay committed to it through thick and thin. Fair enough, but management built around provocative competence does something more. It requires that leaders act with confidence even as they are doubting, questioning, and probing their assumptions.

Provocative leaders develop double vision. They create new narratives while simultaneously understanding that those narratives don't yet fully exist. They invite people to live in hopeful stories. These invitations are not just exercises of the imagination. They demand that people become deeply involved. Provocative leaders are not good listeners in the traditional sense. They don't hear just what's being said. They hear more than what's being said; they "over-listen," hear the overtones of what might emerge, and read more than what is on the page.

As we've just seen, Davis was a transformational leader. He imagined unplayed and overlooked gestures before they existed, and because he did that, the history of jazz and pop music changed forever. So it is with all provocative leaders. They use their double vision to create positive change and inspire alternate possibilities. They introduce a way of talking or acting that doesn't yet exist or even make sense, frequently even to themselves, and they constantly provoke their own understandings by surrounding themselves with people willing to disagree with them, perhaps to the nth degree. To look out over the chaotic and unclear messages in the world and see opportunity, to assume that something of value can be discovered and developed—these are skills to be cherished. Davis did that. Ellington did, too. Business leaders who want to escape an overreliance on automatic processing and familiar routines and dislodge conventional assumptions must do the same.

Perhaps this is what W. L. Gore and Associates, the makers of Gore-Tex, had in mind by abandoning formal job descriptions or conventional chain-of-command reporting structures. When a newly hired MBA reported for work one day, Bill Gore, the president and founder, advised him to "look around and find something you'd like to do." Such a loosely structured environment makes it more difficult to rely on accepted routines and forces new hires to improvise new actions.

Or look at the way in which British Airways encouraged its managers to bring mindfulness to what might have been a routine meeting and imagine instead alternative possibilities heretofore unthinkable. The event was an off-site workshop called to consider ways to improve customer service for business class. However, instead of having participants sleep in regular hotel rooms, one executive had the beds removed and replaced with airline seats. This no doubt disturbed the taken-for-granted routines, not to mention sleep patterns. But, faced with the puzzle of these unexpected constraints, attendees came up with a number of innovations to improve comfort, including the design of a more comfortable seat that included a footrest. In jazz terms, such an irregular arrangement disturbed "stock phrases" and comfortable playing, encouraging members to improvise new solutions.

Then there's the R&D executive at Sony who wanted to create a mini compact disc player but was faced with engineers who had helped develop the original CD technology and were convinced it could not be made more compact. To break the mental logjam, the executive walked into a meeting with a five-inch block of carved wood and told the engineers that the new CD player could be no bigger. The engineers now had novel constraints to work within, a challenging puzzle not unlike the modal sketches that Davis's band members found when they walked into the *Kind of Blue* recording session.

## Nothing Ventured, Nothing Gained

The barriers to provocative competence as a leadership skill are the same as the barriers to personal growth. We become too embedded in our own worldviews. We can't disconnect from the current system, from the notion that there's a "right answer." To grow as a catalyst leader and as a person, we have to be always ready to integrate what we currently are not into our own repertoire. Like improving jazz players, we should be constantly sending out experimental probes to see what kind of responses they attract.

This is essentially what eBay founder Pierre Omidyar did in 1995 when he used his personal Web site to start "Auction Web." He had no idea what items would sell or what kind of response he would get, but he soon discovered that the idea had remarkable attraction—an attraction that developed into eBay. Omidyar never could have developed eBay by starting with market analysis, studying past patterns (because there weren't any), predicting trends, and then creating this product and entering the market based on predictions. It took an experimental move, a probe, to see what would attract responses. Like jazz players, Omidyar had to leap in and take action with no guarantee of what the results would be.

To be sure, leaders risk appearing unrealistic, even foolish, when they make the kinds of leaps that disrupt routines and create stretch goals—the kind of leaps, that is, that provocative competence requires. The data to support such unusual moves simply doesn't exist, nor do the market indicators that would warrant changes in resource allocation and prioritization. Yet without taking such leaps, companies and people remain stuck in the status quo.

Toyota's Lexus LS 400, the first Japanese luxury sedan, is a case in point. Shoichiro Toyoda, son of the company's founder, initially preferred to stick with what Toyota did best—"squeeze water from a dry washcloth" to build "cheap cars for everyman."[15] *Fortune* opined that "getting the Lexus out of Toyota, whose forté is rolling out wheels for the world's millions, is like producing Beef Wellington at McDonald's."[16] When U.S. consumers were asked if they would buy a Japanese luxury car, many replied that "they couldn't even understand the concept of a Japanese luxury car," recounted one Toyota executive—"they thought the term was an oxymoron."[17] But Eiji

Toyoda, president and chairman of Toyota at the time, had a vision of the future, and he practiced provocative competence to build the dynamic capabilities that would get his company there.

To disrupt routine and assemble a heavyweight team, Toyoda issued an intentionally provocative challenge: Lexus "was not to be benchmarked against the 'best car' in the world, but, rather, against every individual best part in the world: the best transmission; the best suspension; the best audio system."[18]

Toyoda demanded that the Lexus LS 400 go from 0 to 60 miles per hour in 7.9 seconds (with a V8 engine, a 4L, 4-cam, 32-valve, fuel-injected motor capable of 250 horsepower) and have a top speed of 150 miles per hour (faster than any of the competition), while being the only luxury car to avoid the gas-guzzler tax by having a fuel efficiency rating of 23.5 miles per gallon. To do so, the LS 400 would have to achieve a drag coefficient of less than .29, where the average luxury car weighed in at .38 to .40 and the average sports car achieved .32. (A Porsche at the time had a drag coefficient of around .30.) *And* this all had to be accomplished while maintaining the design, comfort, quiet, quality, safety, and resale value required to compete with BMW and Mercedes.

Just as Miles Davis had asked his musicians to play a song no one had ever played, in a key no one had ever heard, using a mode that was yet to be invented, so Eiji Toyoda had issued a seemingly impossible challenge that would require unlearning routines in a dramatic way, primarily because the learned responses simply couldn't achieve the goals that had been set. To meet the challenge, employees began experimenting on the margins: the LS 400 evolved from some 450 prototypes, compared to two or perhaps three for the average Toyota, and included thousands of innovations.[19] But setting what at first seemed an unrealistically high bar was clearly worth it. Toyoda's "disruption" resulted in a car that has broken countless records and has been the best-selling luxury automobile in the United States for most of the past decade.

The world of two-wheel transportation offers an equally compelling example of provocative competence at work. By 1998, Giant Manufacturing Company (maker of Giant Bicycles) had become the largest bicycle manufacturer in the world, producing 6.4 million bicycles worldwide. By early 2008, though, the fact that the company's female customers were neither as satisfied nor as profitable as their male counterparts had become personally and painfully evident to Tony Lo, CEO of Giant. In an interview with my colleague and coauthor for a previous book Ethan Bernstein, Lo said:

> *When my wife complained that [Giant] equipment didn't fit her needs, I would say "Okay but do you really need that?" and I would just try to push it off. But you know wives. Even if I kept saying that, it was not enough. She was quite serious. So I tried to find products to suit her needs, and I found that very difficult! And that's only for one woman— the wife of the CEO of the largest bicycle company in the world. Then I discovered that she's not the only one—her, and her friends, and their friends . . . the bicycle has never fit any of their lifestyles. One day I said, "That's enough! I'm going to do something!"*[20]

So, in the midst of continuing success and a worldwide biking boom, Lo set out first to understand the problem and then to utterly remake Giant's approach to the women's market.

Giant had earned the level of frustration that Lo's wife felt. Beginning in the early 2000s, Giant had been systematically leaving women behind as it pushed upmarket in search of profit. As a customer walked in the door, salespeople would first classify him or her as a lifestyle, performance, or sport customer and then customize the sales approach accordingly. The routine aimed to migrate customers upmarket over time, from lifestyle to performance to sport, with significantly increasing margins along the way—a standard best practice in retail.

On sales and profitability metrics, the plan worked wonderfully. Giant was very successfully moving men upmarket. It was not succeeding with women, however. By 2006, several years after implementation of the standardized sales routine, nearly every female customer was still being classified as a lifestyle customer. Giant's retail stores didn't care—their primary interest was in chasing higher-profit, higher-volume customers, and if they were men, so be it. Lo visited a number of stores, only to see the same pattern over and over:

> No one is really paying attention [to women], and even if they wanted to pay attention, they can't. For instance, a bike shop is already crowded . . . it's very difficult for them to squish out even one corner as a women's corner. So what they do is use the same salespeople and treat the sales the same way—the same way they sell to all of the men . . . Even if you go to a pretty good bike store in the U.S., everything is designed for men. The language is for men. Even in the display, women always come in second. All of the models in the window are for men.[21]

In a raw demonstration of provocative competence, Lo saw a strategic opportunity. After exploring the perimeter, his next step was to dislodge habit. Rather than going to the established retail channel for answers, he decided to go straight to the customer: he was convinced that the only way to create a successful business model for women was to open a store exclusively for them. As he put it, "because your only customers are women, if you don't know how to sell to them, you're out of business—period. So you experiment for survival."

Giant's more experienced retail organizations thought Lo was crazy, just as Miles Davis's musicians were bewildered by his provocative moves. Why would corporate open a store exclusively dedicated to its worst (i.e., lowest-profit) customers? In our interview with him, Lo recalled hearing over and over, "Oh, that's a very expensive project! The market is small! And we don't understand women." And Lo admitted that, on every dimension, they were right. Lo recalled the head of Giant Taiwan telling him, "If you twist my arm, I will do it, but it's not for business, so you cannot ask me to make money doing it.

We're just doing it for you." But Lo insisted it be profitable, to which one of the field leaders sarcastically responded, "Well, if that's the case, maybe headquarters should do it!" So Lo, for the sake of openness to whatever lay ahead, did exactly that.

In the process, Lo nurtured an affirmative image. He became an evangelist for the idea, which he claimed was so simple that it was crazy no one had done it successfully. Lo said in retrospect, "When I encountered skeptics, I told them: 'What about women's apparel shops, women's shoes, women's spas, women's fitness clubs?'" And when the skeptics responded that there was no women's car company, Lo pointed out that women and men interfaced with their cars in very similar ways, but with their bikes quite differently, as in the other examples. Each challenge was just an opportunity to learn and refine the concept, and he made sure it wasn't his opportunity alone. In only one year, the special project team of product designers, marketing specialists, and service operations experts had already made "many, many modifications" to the business model. The affirmative image Lo projected provided confidence about Giant's and its employees' ability to be successful.

Lo's approach to the project team demonstrated the last two points of provocative competence: creating situations that demand action, while opening and supporting alternative pathways. Lo picked Bonnie Tu, Giant executive vice president and chief financial officer, to lead the effort—someone with the seniority, reputation, and financial background to marshal resources—and then "*gave her the freedom to break all of the rules.*" Not coincidentally, Tu was the most senior woman at Giant.

Having given Tu the mandate, Lo went a step further, something few CEOs do in similar circumstances: he gave her space to develop any and every option. "There are no limitations," he told her. "It's all your creation; just surprise me. If our women customers are satisfied, then that will be great." Then Lo, who typically checked in on his most important projects daily, told Tu, "see you in six months!" Tu had carte blanche to be entrepreneurial. When Tu decided to replace Giant's typical central store fixture—a display with Giant's latest and greatest bicycle—with a comfortable, chocolate-color leather couch, Lo simply smiled in approval.

Lo's smile substantially broadened, however, when the Liv/giant store, Giant's first all-women's store in downtown Taipei, turned profitable only four months after its grand opening. Even after incurring nearly twice the opening costs of a typical Giant store, this was one of the fastest paths to profitability in Giant's retail history. Everything about the store had been designed to be as modular as possible to optimize Giant's ability to experiment, learn, and innovate. Its all-women clientele, 80 percent of whom became repeat customers, appreciated the effort more than anyone could have predicted. The improvisation encouraged by the provocative competence of a leader like Lo had substantially paid off. When we last talked to Lo, his greatest problem was deciding where to open the next all-women's stores, while still finding time to ride with his wife, who had already purchased three bicycles—first lifestyle, then performance, and now sport—from Taipei's flagship Liv/giant store.

## Jumping Evolution

Would something like the Lexus 400 LS eventually have arrived on the automotive scene? Would another bike manufacturer have finally filled the void for female customers? How about *Kind of Blue*? Its uniqueness can never be recovered, but would an album just as revolutionary have ever been cut? The answer in all three cases is almost certainly yes. Market conditions were clearly ripe for a top-of-the-line (in all regards) Japanese luxury sedan and for a bike-buying experience and environment that was more gender-specific. *Kind of Blue* broke the mold, but in the arts, the mold is always being shattered in one way or another, with varying degrees of success. A million monkeys at a million typewriters would never write one of Shakespeare's plays, but they might well come up with one of his play's first lines.

What is singular about each of these examples is that the principals—Eiji Toyada, Tony Lo, and Miles Davis (and by extension Duke Ellington)—jumped the evolutionary process. They didn't wait for a product or an idea to become inevitable or unavoidable. All of them had visions of something better on the horizon. All disrupted routine to enable their team to get there. They affirmed the best in those who worked for them. They raised the bar high and demanded activity—but always to achieve worthwhile goals—and they allowed those they provoked to competence and beyond to proceed incrementally.

In a more global sense, these leaders also chose what parts of the organization to nurture and refine. They created organizational designs, structures, tasks, and a culture that encouraged improvisation in the right locations. Also, they were careful to preserve organizational memory—to maintain those routines that are crucial and retain practices that should not be abandoned. Change isn't about blowing everything up; that's chaos and headlines. Change that endures is about designing organizational structures to sustain successful existing procedures while simultaneously triggering improvisation and creativity beyond existing capabilities.

Routine times don't always reward rote processes and routine thinking, but at least they don't punish them too severely. Times such as we now live in—chaotic markets, ever-shifting price points, almost instantaneous duplication, and absolutely assured obsolescence—call for a different mode of leadership, one that transcends conventional practices and traditional assumptions.

CHAPTER EIGHT

# Getting to "Yes to the Mess"

## Advancing Engaged, Strategic Improvisation

In late 2010, IBM conducted a massive interview study, with over fourteen hundred CEOs from sixty nations and thirty-three industries taking part. In the midst of the worst economic crisis in several generations, IBM asked this small army of corporate generals to talk about the dilemmas they faced in managing their companies. Did they wish their top people had more discipline, more rigor, a better hand on operations, a higher commitment to integrity and ethics? Were their companies squandering resources? Did they need a better grasp of globalization or more intimacy with the customer? All these issues arose, but the one quality these CEOs valued above all others was creativity: over 60 percent rated it as the most important leadership trait.[1] They agreed that innovation is the crucial capability.

At one level, this shouldn't come as much of a surprise. Organizations such as Starbucks, Google, Facebook, and Amazon show that even in the face of unprecedented challenges, innovation wins the day. Yet, often the same CEOs who so value creativity go to great effort to create the impression that improvisation does not happen in organizations. They and their top managers construct plans and organization charts, offer training, and perform drills that are designed to both anticipate the unexpected and minimize unnecessary idiosyncratic actions and deviations from formal pathways. What's more, the after-action stories that leaders tell tend to paint responses to the unexpected as measured, deliberative, and rational, when the reality is that the players involved were experimenting ad hoc all over the place.

As I hope this book has shown, real people in real organizations are constantly jumping into action without clear plans, making up reasons as they proceed, discovering new routes once action is initiated, proposing multiple interpretations, navigating through discrepancies, combining disparate and incomplete materials, and then discovering what their original purpose was after the fact. There's no getting around the fact that managers have to improvise. The good news is that they can learn to do it even better.

*Yes to the Mess* is not a call to get rid of routines and structures. Organizations need both. Studies of project teams show that many problems managers face can, in fact, be confronted successfully with preplanned routines and structures. The problem comes when companies overrely on structured responses, especially in situations where a different kind of thinking is needed. Those situations occur only episodically within any organization, but they are often moments of the greatest consequence—when 80 percent of effects, as the Pareto Principle holds, result from 20 percent of the causes. Those are the situations in which you want your organization to function less like a well-programmed machine and more like Duke Ellington's orchestra at the Cotton Club or Miles Davis's quintet recording *Kind of Blue*. The crucial question that leaders should ask: How can you design conditions so that teams and organizations "hit the groove"—a dynamic synchronization in which members are attuned to one another, learning and executing simultaneously? Organizations that hit the groove allow people to achieve personal growth and learn even while work-ing.They pay attention to the mental models that enable and accelerate learning, creating cultures that foster experimentation, and designing structures that encourage attunement to what unfolds. And then they drive these mental models deep into their own organizations.

## Improviser's Toolkit

The clear premise of this book is that nurturing spontaneity, creativ-ity, experimentation, and dynamic synchronization is no longer an optional approach to leadership. It's the *only* approach. The current velocity of change demands nothing less. It demands paying attention to the mental models, the cultural beliefs and values, the practices and structures that support improvisation.

Following are eleven practices and structures that can help your organization emulate what happens when jazz bands improvise.

### 1. Approach leadership tasks as experiments.

Business gurus would have us believe that the essence of leadership can be captured in a list—the seven qualities of great leaders, the five steps to leading change, and so on. But leadership is much more compli-cated and unpredictable than that. Even when leaders find a solution that gets the desired results, it is only a temporary landing spot. Given the pace and depth of change, leaders have no choice but to improvise. Perhaps the greatest contribution a leader can make to any organiza-tion today is building competency in anticipation and adaptation.

How to accomplish that? By approaching tasks as experiments. When you approach leadership actions in this way, you are uncommonly receptive to what emerges, *and* you heighten self-awareness while in the middle of taking action. By definition, successful experimentation requires suspending a defensive attitude. In paying close attention to your own experience, you notice the constraint of your own bias as well as the nuances and gradations of others' responses.

An experimental approach favors testing and learning as you go. It means presenting ideas, then observing how others pick up and build on them. This is leadership with a mind-set of discovery, floating hypotheses about what might work and what might not, and leaving both the hypotheses and yourself open to contradictory data and recalcitrant forces. You might run several experiments simultaneously, testing various programs and approaches to see what works and extracting lessons to fashion your next moves.

Being experimental does not mean you have to be overly tentative. Anyone who has a leadership role needs to have an air of authority. But there's no way of knowing all that could or might happen, and it's too easy to get stuck in analysis paralysis. Sometimes it's necessary to just leap in and act. When you start acting, new possibilities emerge. Horizons expand and pathways appear that you could not have anticipated during prior planning.

Consider Napoleon's strategy as an example. When Napoleon moved his understaffed, hungry, and ill-supplied army into Italy, opposing forces divided to thwart him. The Austrians defended Milan; the Italian army moved to defend Turin. Rather than attack one of the major cities as conventional strategy dictated, Napoleon moved between them, and the confused Italians sent troops out to find him. This allowed Napoleon to fight smaller numbers of troops in smaller towns throughout the region. The towns themselves were not strategically important. He simply fought the troops where he found them.

The Austrians drew more tightly around Milan, expecting Napoleon to attack there, but Napoleon responded by bypassing Milan all together. Fearing that he might be heading toward their homeland, the Austrians left Milan to go after him. Reckoning that the Austrians would have to cross the Adda River at the town of Lodi, Napoleon set up his artillery and waited, not knowing for sure what the enemy would do or where they would appear. Then as the Austrians crossed the bridge, he fired upon them and ultimately defeated them. This was all ad hoc strategy. Like a great jazz musician, Napoleon acted first, saw what emerged, and *then* took focused action.[2]

Rather than over-rely on preplanned strategies and canonical job descriptions, leaders need to acknowledge peoples' capacity for bricolage and pragmatic reasoning as well as their ability to juxtapose, recombine, and reinterpret past materials to fashion novel responses. Organizational learning, then, must be seen as a risky venture, as you reach into the unknown with no guarantee of where your explorations will lead.

Questions leaders can ask:

> How can you encourage people to see leadership as a set of learning experiments?

> How can you make it safe for people to take thoughtful risks?

> Can you think of a time you surprised yourself by leaping in and trying something new, even though there was no guarantee of the outcome? Have you shared such stories with others?

> When have you encouraged people to explore novel responses?

> Where else in your organization can you encourage people to leap in and experiment, to adjust on the spot rather than waiting for a plan or sticking with safe routines?

### 2. Boost information processing in the midst of action.

Jazz players act their way into the future, then justify their actions by placing their statements within a context of meaning. It's only by looking back at what they have created, for example, that jazz soloists realize how the notes, phrases, and chords relate. Organizations can use the same sort of after-action review to help people become aware of the goals and values they implicitly hold and what constraints these values place upon their future actions. Sharing the multiple interpretations of diverse participants close to the action helps everyone involved retrospectively make sense of or construct a story or justification for what they have already done. These stories then can become the seeds for greater discoveries and inventions.

To boost their own processing of information, organizations might consider a strategic orientation that links planning, action, implementation, and environmental scanning. Think about creating virtual strategic planning sessions in which members engage in trial-and-error thinking, just as jazz musicians do when they solo. Generating multiple, simultaneous alternatives minimizes escalation of commitment to a single option and allows members to make adjustments and reorientations on the fly as feedback comes in. This view challenges the traditional notion of strategic planning as a form of rational control, or as an abstract exercise divorced from and prior to action.

In this spirit, Peter Senge has advocated a view of planning as play, or as "practice fields" in which managers practice thinking ahead, predicting, and guessing future moves within various constraints.[3] In virtual planning scenarios, managers could try out alternative maps and alter the core assumptions that have remained unquestioned.[4] Arie de Geus recounts the experience of managers at Shell Oil who were asked to respond to multiple (and sometimes contradictory) assumptions about their environmental constraints, including entertaining the notion that the price of oil might be slashed in half—something that seemed unthinkable at the time (and still does). This became, in de Geus's words, a "license to play." These incremental disruptions created a larger repertoire of action scenarios, so when an unprecedented event did occur, Shell managers were prepared to respond.[5]

Nancy Katz notes that Don Shula, the Hall of Fame coach of the Miami Dolphins, followed the common NFL practice of having his team watch game video on Mondays—or Tuesday for a featured Monday night tilt. But Shula took the ritual several steps further. The Dolphins would watch the film at various times throughout the week and in different groups, including odd combinations of players who normally did not work together but, because of that, might notice nuances and subtleties that a predictable combination might miss. The unusual groupings also provided a venue for players to notice one another's contributions in a way that wasn't possible during the heat of the game. Katz writes, "It was an opportunity for an offensive star like Dan Marino to notice and comment on a great hit by a defensive player who rarely got the limelight."[6]

There is much to be learned from these debriefing sessions, hearing what others experienced, how they felt, what they noticed, and what they learned. Take time to gather intelligence; go over which routines worked and which didn't; examine which behaviors triggered desired outcomes, what it felt like to take risks, and how members felt supported or abandoned by one another. The U.S. Marines call these "hot-wash" sessions, in which everyone reflects on what they did that worked and didn't work, and what to do differently next time. Hot-wash your own organization.

> How can you create spaces for people to tell stories about what they are doing in their work, a chance to share learning experiences and insights?

> How can you create opportunities for people to entertain various scenarios and future possibilities?

### 3. Prepare for serendipity by deliberately breaking a routine.

Routines in organizations and in jazz bands can drive out serendipity and discovery. Reliable routines are necessary to achieve efficiency, and some simply can't be toyed with. But every organization supports at least a few routines that have become competency traps in which people remain loyal to specific practices even when the practices are no longer useful. Too often, managers have been trained to eliminate variation and deviation at all costs and so drive out creativity.

Serendipity doesn't just happen. I hope I've shown that it takes preparation. Work teams are particularly vulnerable to falling into a pattern of activity without explicitly thinking about it or deciding to do so. Even a simple process question in the midst of team activity can serve to disrupt routines just enough to trigger people to consider options: "I'm thinking we should talk about what we're doing here. What if we try something else?" This kind of statement is a small way to break up a practice that might have become habituated and is handicapping performance outside of anyone's awareness.

Generous listening might be the core factor that allows you to escape the seduction of outworn routines and automatic habits. Jay Parks, a veteran New York actor, told me about the challenge of keeping each performance fresh. Imagine that you're delivering the same lines each night, eight times each week for fifty weeks. How can you keep your performance fresh? Parks was clear that the secret is what happens *before* you say your lines—in the way you relate to your fellow actors. In order to avoid automatic pilot mode, you need to be open and receptive to those around you. It's all about listening.

"The only way the changes and freshness in a performance happen is by listening to what is being said each time the lines are spoken instead of just waiting to say your next line," Parks told me. "If one truly listens, the delivery of a line is different every night, and thus the response is different each time." That applies pretty much to everyone's life. You can choose to "disrupt a routine" by paying attention (listening) to the moment at hand and realizing that "routine" is a choice. Do I do it the same boring way each time, or do I choose to make it fresh and new?

This set of skills is different from those usually taught in business schools. Most MBA programs and organizations encourage leaders to articulate an inspiring vision, communicate clearly, and analyze market trends accurately—all important skills to be sure. But imagine if MBA programs began to emphasize the kind of skills that jazz musicians and actors like Parks discuss. What would be the effect of an MBA program that emphasized—or an organization that assessed its leaders on—the skills of receptivity, listening generously, acceptance, presence, openness, assent, and affirmation?

The caveat to this, of course, is that there's a big difference between deliberately breaking a routine and allowing routines to decay or drift because of inattention. Scott Snook's study of army Black Hawk helicopters shot down by air force F-15s over Iraq on a routine patrol found that both organizations had plans and procedures that were gradually ignored as different units began to modify the routines and take shortcuts and work-arounds. These local improvisations began to drift farther away from the conditions needed for safety, and the implementers and original planners lost touch. The moral: groups creating local improvisations need to stay in touch with those making global plans and procedures, so that planning, policy, and implementation do not drift too far apart.

Questions leaders can ask:

> Where have you seen a routine or habit that has outlived its usefulness and has blocked the flow of good ideas or good execution?

> What routines do you notice that need to be deliberately disrupted so as to open the possibility of new thinking and the search for innovative solutions?

> What can you do to help others unlearn their tacitly held beliefs and practices so that they (and *you*) can move beyond the limitations of accepted ways of doing things?

### 4. Expand the vocabulary of *yes* to overcome the glamour of *no*.

One of the biggest blocks to creativity and improvisation is getting stuck wishing the situation was different. Telling yourself, "If only I could get off this team" or "Why did I get stuck with this set of tools and these people?" shuts down improvisation. Instead, do what jazz greats do: assume that you can make the situation work *somehow*, that there exists an opportunistic possibility to be gleaned. This is an affirmative mind-set—the assumption that a positive pathway will be found, that there's a potential to be noticed and pursued.

Too often, in established cultures, cynicism is a way to attain status, and cynical responses to ideas seem justified because they are more "realistic." It is much easier to critique than to build. The word "no" has seductive glamour and richly nuanced grammar and vocabulary. Saying "no" to proposals feels less risky than saying "yes" or offering affirmative support. If you affirm possibilities for which the rationale may be incomplete or unclear, you may risk being seen as unrealistic or, worse, Pollyannaish. Yet equating cynicism with realism shrinks the imagination. Too often, executives become far more adept at critiquing others' ideas than they are at creating their own original ideas or lending support to those of others.

What we need is a corresponding expansive grammar of "yes," a rich repertoire of affirmative moves or responses that convey the tacit assurance that we will help each other think through ideas, that our initiatives will not be overly constrained by unnecessary structures, that our moves will be a positive contribution, and that possibilities will unfold and glimpses of wider potential horizon will emerge.

Saying yes is a way of moving forward, yet can be psychologically risky. There are no guarantees that you will be able to proceed safely. You may be with people you don't know well or who do not have the skills to provide a safety net as you go out on a limb. And some people might be working out emotional or psychological problems by treating an issue as a kind of game and "seeing what happens." All these factors make having a bias for yes a delicate matter, but research has shown that people flourish when they are affirmed.

Rather than indulge in easy "noes," executives need to help groups to identify, analyze, and amplify positive deviance. Celebrate even small successes and early wins. Team members who experience even the possibility of success will expect more from each other. Also, they are likely to have more faith in their teammates' skills and their own capacity as a collective.

At the macro level, you should encourage the flourishing of a richer grammar of "yes" to honor the power of the imagination. To this end, the capacity to envision where an idea or action might lead and to rouse ideas to life even before they have come to full fruition is central. You would do well to activate your own imagination and legitimize others' imaginative activities as well. New ideas are fragile and lack solid evidence, so people need the capacity to visualize and to make scenarios come alive so that they can more easily discern what might work. If you kindle imagination in others and stir possibility, you are likely to create an improvisation-rich culture, one in which people are led naturally to self-discovery.

Questions leaders can ask:

How can you expand the vocabulary of "yes" in your organization? How can you deliberately highlight the positive potential in nascent ideas that have yet to achieve fruition?

Where have you or others seen an obstacle and turned it into an opportunity?

When have you engaged in appreciative inquiry?

How can you inquire into positive deviance or epiphanies that have lead to innovative action?

How can you help your organization create a vocabulary of "yes," a stronger repertoire of positivity? For example, how can you look for opportunities to ask how your group or organization is functioning when people are at their best? Can you encourage people to talk about moments of exceptional meaning, full engagement in their work, or experiences of high purpose and self-worth?

### 5. Take advantage of the clunkers.

To get to yes, leaders need to create a culture that doesn't rebuke people for admitting mistakes and that values failure as a potent source for learning. This doesn't mean all failures are alike or somehow ultimately good, but you need to acknowledge and distinguish thoughtful experimentation from carelessness. Errors are a chance to look at the assumptions behind the original action; failures can provide data and insight that are unavailable by any other means. The challenge is to distinguish between mistakes that are a failure of genuine, thoughtful effort and mistakes that are a failure of thoughtful experimentation.

The important first step is to level status differences so that people feel safe to experiment. Leaders have to actively let others see them as learners and therefore should be among the first to admit mistakes. Doing so announces to all that errors are indispensable in the creative process and creates an aesthetic of imperfection and forgiveness that construes errors as a source of learning that can open new lines of inquiry.

A further way that managers can help teams and individuals benefit from failures is to discern two different kinds of learning—about ourselves and about the situation—both of which are valuable. Imagine I am working with a client and fashioning an organizational change intervention. When I try something and make a mistake, I learn something about myself and what I could have done differently, how my own beliefs and current methods biased the way we gathered information, how my assumptions were misplaced, and how I had a bias when I favored one strategy over another. That's invaluable information, but it's also important to go beyond this lesson and notice what else has been revealed about the situation itself. In this case, I also have learned something important about the client—what the client does not like and what triggers resistance and at what level. Both forms of learning through failure are crucial for shaping future intervention strategies and should be embedded in the culture of the organization.

Questions leaders can ask:

When has "getting it right no matter what" gotten in the way of learning from failure?

How can you further the belief that both success *and* failure generate useful data that stimulates learning?

When have you learned from a failure yet failed to let others know about it?

What can you do to lower status differences so that it becomes safe for others to admit and learn from their mistakes?

Since the consequences of action are by nature often unpredictable, what can you do to create an aesthetic of forgiveness in your organization?

How are you making it safe for interpersonal risktaking?

When is the last time you praised someone who dissented from you, demonstrating to others that alternative perspectives are valuable?

### 6. Ensure that everyone has a chance to solo from time to time.

When self-directed work teams are performing well, they are often characterized by distributed, multiple leadership in which people take turns heading up various projects as their expertise is needed. The same happens in jazz bands, where everyone gets a turn to solo. In both instances, though, there exists the problem of influential members who might control or dominate a group.

A simple organizational development tool called the nominal group technique is structured to avoid just this issue: Every individual in turn brainstorms out loud, while others listen to his or her ideas. No one is allowed to interrupt or redirect; instead, people are encouraged to build on other ideas they have heard.[7] A variation of this approach is to require that no one speaks twice until every other person in the group speaks at least once. This is an impersonal, non-negotiable structure that monitors airtime, cultivates group creativity, and ensures that every individual has a voice. Every now and then, let your talented people run free. Google and 3M both understand this. Both organizations thrive through innovation because they encourage their employees to solo, to take 20 percent of their time to engage in any project that they think will help the company and that they are passionate about.

Letting everyone solo from time to time means releasing them from group identity stereotypes, giving them full voice, and making sure that others take them seriously. That can be hard work for a manager, but when you hold open the possibility that the converse of every proposition is equally valid, you also get to reframe your current belief and stay humble. Think of something that you feel very strongly about, something that is somewhat controversial, or something with which others might disagree, and run a thought trial in which you assume that the opposite assumptions are valid. What new connotations are now imaginable?

Questions to ask yourself:

> What can you do to make room for multiple voices and perspectives within your system? How can you assure that it is safe to articulate diverse views and that they are taken seriously by others?

> When have you last seen people support one another, help each other to think out loud, to experiment, to take a risk with an unproven idea?

### 7. Celebrate comping to create a culture of noble followership.

What happens when you actively acknowledge that you need others to complete your thinking? Not only do you learn humility, you also ennoble the contribution of others.

As mentioned earlier, organizations need to go beyond merely inviting new voices. They also must create processes that suspend the tendency to criticize, judge, and express the sort of disbelief that might kill a nascent idea. But what's the opposite of all that? What roles and behaviors can we nurture in people so that they support, affirm, and commit to helping each other be more expressive? Here again jazz provides a model: comping.

Organizations can achieve comping by supporting behaviors such as mentoring, advocating, encouraging, and listening. This means rewarding those who support other people's opportunity to take center stage, including blending and helping them along the way as they transition and develop ideas at different rates. To get there, leaders need to expand their stories about creative achievements beyond highlighting individual autonomous action to include the roles of those who assisted, who made room, and who encouraged fledgling, nascent gestures with subtle nudges, just as a jazz pianist does with his (or her) comping.

When they comp, jazz musicians agree to suspend judgment, to trust that whatever the soloist is doing right now will lead to something, to blend into the flow and direction of the idea rather than to break off in an independent direction. Such democratic structures enhance the likelihood that people have not only the right to be heard, but also the opportunity to influence.

Questions to ask:

> What can you do in your organization to acknowledge efforts to help each other be successful?

> When have you last seen people support one another and help each other think out loud, experiment, or take a risk with an unproven idea?

> How can you reward people for helping others be successful rather than simply rewarding their individual achievements?

> When have you last actively acknowledged that you rely on others' input to improve or complete your thinking?

### 8. Create minimal structures that maximize autonomy.

Organizations understandably favor structures like reporting procedures, deadlines, and the like because they ease a manager's anxiety and satisfy her need to know that something is being accomplished. But these structures also can quell positive deviance and drive out creativity. The key is to find the delicate balance between constraint and the chance to vary from standard operating procedures.

In the same vein, we often hear about the importance of creating consensus in organizations. True, it is important for groups and organizations to have widespread agreement—to have "everyone on board" and everyone "reading on the same page." Here again, though, an improvisation mind-set suggests that too much consensus is as dangerous as no consensus because it drives out variety and diverse ideas. Instead of guarding against dissent and debate, you should value them for their potential. The key is to have just enough consensus and to have consensus on the core of what matters, rather than seek clarity and agreement on every principle. Ambiguity can be generative.

Part of attending to minimal structures means noticing group rhythm, when moments of convergence and divergence are happening or, more importantly, when they are necessary. Research has shown that when teams face a deadline, they have one special moment, the naturally occurring midpoint of the group project, when they become peculiarly open to learning, revising, and recommitting.[8] The midpoint offers a way for the group to pace itself, as members stop to notice how they are doing, what is working, and what they need to do to accomplish the task as the deadline looms.

Balance is the key. If leaders try to create too much structure by demanding that the group report progress at arbitrary times, they are likely to meet resistance or reap mere compliance rather than a genuine moment of reframing and learning. This might further suggest that managers create a minimal structure that calls for a reflective time-out at the halfway point of a group project. Or they might impose a few significant deadlines as a way of creating more midpoints and thus more meaningful learning and reflection along the way.

Questions to ask:

> What pivots and markers do you have in place to update
> and inspire each other about ongoing contributions, insights,
> experiments, and findings?

> What are the core minimal values and vision that are non-
> negotiable, to which all must adhere so that all are free to
> embellish, branch out, respond, and innovate?

### 9. Encourage serious play. Too much control inhibits flow.

As we have seen, jazz is an activity marked by paradox: musicians must
balance structure and freedom, autonomy and interdependence, surrender and control. They grapple with the constrictions of previous
patterns and structures. They strive to listen and respond to what is
happening; at the same time, they try to break out from these patterns to do something new, with all the risks that both paths entail.
If musicians strive too much to hit a groove, achieve flow, or jam, they
obstruct it.[9]

Organizational theorists have articulated a similar paradox. As
Robert Quinn argues: "When behaving with conscious purpose,
people tend to act upon the environment, not with it."[10]

One way to manage this paradox is to adopt the same disciplined
concentration you use when playing a game. There is a sense of surrender in play, a willingness to suspend control and give yourself over to
the flow of the ongoing events. Organizations like Southwest Airlines try
to encourage much the same when they declare that having fun in the
workplace is a core value. In effect, they question the conventional sepa-
ration between work and play and recognize that legitimate play can be a
fruitful, meaningful activity, one that enhances the sheer joy of relational
activity. Play and practice are places where it's OK to experiment and fail.
This is one reason IDEO's motto is "Fail often, so you'll succeed sooner."
We might amend that to "Play often, so that you might execute better."[11]

Managers might even consider calling play "time-outs"—that is, creating a protective space around the teams and/or individuals with enough bounded safety so that members can experiment with new ideas. When performing for perfect execution, it's harder to feel the necessary freedom to consider multiple data points and entertain different scenarios. Anxiety inevitably mounts, and research has demonstrated that high anxiety inhibits learning. Playtime, by contrast, is learning time. Imagine what might happen if a manager had monthly or quarterly play sessions in which space and time were carved out for experimenting with alternative procedures.

> How can you create space and cultivate serious play in your organization?
>
> What can you do to lessen anxiety to support ongoing learning and collaboration in your organization?

## 10. Jam.

We talk about ideas as if they happen to us in instants, like a flash of insight. However, as Steven Johnson has pointed out, ideas emerge when people interact in diverse, stimulating networks, among people with varied backgrounds and different expertise.[12] Or as Steve Jobs once said, creativity comes from spontaneous meetings and random discussions: "You run into someone, you ask what they're doing, you say 'Wow,' and soon you're cooking up all sorts of ideas."[13] What better model for that than jamming, whose very essence is hanging out, sharing stories, tossing around musical ideas, and thinking out loud— and sometimes very out loud?

Good ideas can come from several different sources, including those outside the accepted boundaries of an organization. The conventional model we've grown up with proposes that manufacturers identify the needs of users, develop products, and gain profit by protecting and selling the goods they have developed. But if we include users and customers in our jam sessions, the field of ideas expands almost exponentially. Users, after all, have good ideas. They commonly know how to solve their needs and are often intrinsically willing to share their insights and innovations. Eric von Hippel found multiple examples of the products of such uber-jamming, among them mountain bikes, Gatorade, and new medical devices for those who had suffered spinal injuries.[14] In each of these examples, it was users, not manufacturers or engineering designers, who came up with the initial innovations. Ideas can come from anywhere, but they won't be heard if organizations don't create a jamming space that welcomes and branches out with these ideas.

LEGO Mindstorms—a computer brain—is a case in point. LEGO originally joined forces with MIT Labsto to build a programmable robot for the retail market, but that was only the beginning of the creative process. Shortly after the product was released in 1998, hackers created several software programs to further program the robots. Within a very short time, more users began to create sensors and peripherals that could be combined and used to upgrade the robot capabilities. When it was ready to create the next generation—Mindstorms NXT—LEGO asked its users and customers directly to help them design the new product.

Over time, this strong community of practice has grown to include professionals and hobbyists who share their innovations in design, programming, and software. The community has created a Web site on which LEGO itself encourages people to share their own codes and download those of others. So successful has the process been that the company now has a wiki to support user involvement. In truth, Duke Ellington himself couldn't have created a better jam session.[15]

Questions to ask:

> Where in your organization are the open times or casual places that allow for "happy accidents," serendipitous exchanges, fruitful conversations, and curious questions?

Should you be sponsoring open forums for people to discuss ideas freely and analyze nascent ideas and discuss results from experimenting?

What else could you do to foster informal, in-house learning from others' activities?

### 11. Cultivate provocative competence: create expansive promises as occasions for stretching out into unfamiliar territory.

The mental models I have just been describing do flatten status within organizations, but they don't diminish the role of leadership. In fact, the need of leadership in a distributed age has never been greater. Instead of *imposing* competence—a virtual impossibility—leaders *provoke* it by designing the conditions that nurture strategic improvisation and continuous learning, and thus help their organizations break out of competency traps. Great leaders like Miles Davis are able to see peoples' potential, disrupt their habits, and demand that they pay attention in new ways.

One common learning obstacle in organizations occurs when managers choose to address only those problems that are familiar and those issues for which a solution is imaginable.[16] Miles Davis did just the opposite. He surprised his band by stretching them beyond comfortable limits, calling unrehearsed songs and familiar songs in foreign keys so that they would have to experiment in the margins. That's provocative competence at work.

One way leaders can encourage provocative competence is by evoking a set of higher values and ideals that inspire passionate engagement. Visionary organizations make expansive promises that defy reasonable limits and thus stretch members to redefine the boundaries of what they have experienced as constraining.

Provocative competence is much more than simply disrupting people; it involves calibrating the size of the challenge you issue.

A provocation that is too much or too overwhelming threatens self-efficacy and will have deleterious effect on performance. You also have to remain after the disruption and support the inevitable starts and stops. Leaders know that it's important not to hold on too tightly or let a provocation go too far off the deep end.

Provocative competence is well served, too, by a selective memory, one that allows you to focus on who people are when they are at their best. That way, you'll feel more comfortable disrupting the routines of your reports, knowing that their potential likely will shine through in spite of the temporary chaos. Whatever the immediate outcome, though, the long-term benefit is worth the risk. Provocative competence does nothing less than rouse minds to life.

Questions to ask:

> When have you last noticed the edge of peoples' comfort level and encouraged them to go beyond the familiar?

> How are people in our organization "playing it safe" by repeating what has worked in the past?

> When have you last noticed anyone stretching competence by edging around his or her own comfort level?

> Have you deliberately paid attention to who people are when they are operating at their best, even though they might have forgotten it themselves?

> Have you been able to remember who they are at their best even thought they might not always be performing at that level?

> Can you imagine an incremental disruption that might dislodge peoples' habits and demand that they respond in new ways?

> Yes, this is leadership largely without hierarchy, but it is also leadership at its best and most creative.

## The Improvising Organization

What would an organization look like if it valued these points and sought to learn from jazz bands? Managers, for starters, would have a high respect for emergent strategy, and they would be careful not to separate those formulating strategy from those in charge of implementation, because action creates feedback that informs the next step. To that end, top management would be in the field learning about the changing environment and getting hands-on concrete experience on a regular basis.

The improvising organization would create fluid structures that form, dissolve, and reform as new situations and challenges arise. Project groups would not be started as the result of *a priori* abstract planning sessions but emerge as the situation requires. Groups would come and go, assembled to address issues and serve specific functions and then dissolved.

Strategy would be created retrospectively as people try something, form groups to discuss it, and then articulate what the strategy was. People from different functional specialties would talk to one another regularly, sharing insights and expertise as the situation demands. Wide-eyed expressions would be commonplace as insights popped up from unlikely places at unpredictable times and as workers arrived at new understanding through collaborative processes.

Organizations would create minimal guidelines, allowing employees to orient themselves to concrete situations and follow their hunches to make contributions as needed. Energy would ebb and flow, as individuals and groups followed their passions or responded to an adaptive challenge. There would be a sense of joint discovery as people struggle with situations that are tough to grasp, working out ideas and considering options, discovering new possibilities only after tentative action is already initiated. Top-down mandates would be greeted with suspicion if not ignored for fear that they might drive out these bottom-up negotiations and sense-making processes.

Rather than being isolated silo by silo, employees would work on multiple projects at the same time and be members of several overlapping teams. Cross-silo conversations and interactions would create a conversational mode built around curiosity. Inquiry sentences would pepper the air: Where did that come from? How did you find that out? Why am I the only one who didn't seem to have known this? Why didn't we figure this out earlier? Why? Not because everyone wanted to act the expert but because workers would never be quite satisfied with what they know, never completely confident that they are prepared for what is going to happen next.

Since meaning and scenarios would be fluid, people would rely less on cognitive clarity and would be more comfortable with uncertainty and ambiguity. It would be easier to admit what you don't know and to feel free to draw upon others for help in getting information, and easier also to move into whatever role required at the moment the need arises. One hotel chain that wanted to emphasize four-star service in which all personnel were responsible for delighting the customer simply got rid of job titles altogether. All employees were henceforth "associates," equally expected to respond to requests regardless of whether they fit into preordained departmental requirements.

This is what an improv organization would be all about. Trespassing would be forgiven, even occasionally encouraged, in the sense that people would be willing to take on extra responsibility beyond traditional roles. At Roadway Trucking, where line-level employees are deeply involved in strategic planning, truck drivers didn't wait for approval to get cell phones so they could communicate important information about their shipment loads and delivery times. Rather, they went out and bought the phones themselves, and then started using them to demonstrate that these important resources should be funded in department budgets.

"Everyone doing everything"—that's a good motto for jazz bands and for organizations that want to learn to improvise.

I don't want to overidealize jazz bands or jazz itself. In reality, not all players are equally competent. No amount of listening, support, or comping can enhance a performance if the musician is not up to the task. Performers of lesser competence can have a debilitating effect on overall group performance. The same is true in business. While tolerance of errors is essential to enhance experimentation, there are cases where errors are intolerable—in high-reliability organizations, for example.

That said, I hope I have shown in this book that jazz improvisation is a strikingly useful model for understanding and improving organizations interested in learning and innovation. To be innovative, managers—like jazz musicians—must interpret vague cues, face unstructured tasks, process incomplete knowledge, *and* take action anyway. Both managers and jazz players need to engage in dialogue and negotiation, and the creation of shared spaces for decision making based on expertise rather than hierarchical position. Jazz performances are not haphazard or accidental. Musicians prepare themselves to be spontaneous. Managers and executives can do the same, so that their organizations can learn and act simultaneously.

Finally, jazz improvisation should be seen as a hopeful and empowering activity. It models individual actors as protean agents capable of changing the shape and flow of events. In this sense, jazz holds an appreciative view of human potential: it represents belief in the human capacity to think freshly, to generate novel solutions, and to create something new and interesting, perhaps even transformative.[17] All leaders and organizations should aspire to such a view.

# NOTES

## Preface

1. F. J. Barrett, "Creativity and Improvisation in Jazz and Organizations: Implications for Organizational Learning," *Organization Science* 9 (1998): 605–622. This article was the inspiration and model for this book.

## Chapter 1

1. P. Drucker, *The New Realities* (New York: Harper and Row, 1989).

2. K. Weick, "Improvisation as a Mindset for Organizational Analysis," *Organization Science* 9, no. 5 (1998): 543–555.

3. Quoted in P. Berliner, *Thinking in Jazz* (Chicago: University of Chicago Press, 1994), 102.

4. M. Gridley, *Jazz Styles* (Englewood Cliffs, NJ: Prentice-Hall, 1991), 302, 303.

5. D. Bailey, *Improvisation* (New York: Da Capo Press, 1992), 57.

6. See http://www.youtube.com/watch?v=cCvLTlQWT6A&NR=1.

7. T. Gioia, *The Imperfect Art* (New York: Oxford University Press, 1988).

8. See http://www.nytimes.com/2010/12/05/business/05ge.html?pagewanted=all.

9. D. Carr, *Keith Jarrett* (New York: Da Capo Press, 1991).

10. Bailey, *Improvisation*, 51.

11. A. Hamilton and L. Konitz, *Conversations on the Improviser's Art* (Ann Arbor: University of Michigan Press, 2007), 103.

12. R. S. Tedlow, *Andy Grove: The Life and Times of an American* (New York: Portfolio, 2006); and A. Grove, *Only the Paranoid Survive* (New York: Crown Business, 1996), 89.

13. A. Grove, *Only the Paranoid Survive*.

14. See http://www.newyorker.com/archive/2005/01/17/050117fa_fact.

## Chapter 2

1. J. M. O'Brien, "Amazon's Next Revolution," *Fortune*, May 26, 2009.

2. T. Gioia, *The Imperfect Art* (New York: Oxford University Press, 1988).

3. For an intriguing example of an organization that developed through bricolage, see Tom Szaky, *Revolution in a Bottle: How TerraCycle is Redefining Green Business* (New York: Portfolio, 2009). This book tells the story of how Szaky founded a company that recycles garbage into poop worm, liquefies it, and packages it

in used soda bottles. It is an inspiring story of learning by serendipity, taking advantage of the material at hand to put together an innovative ecobusiness model.

4. For an excellent description of the comedy improviser's art along with applications to the business world, see P. Meyer, *From Workplace to Playspace: Innovating, Learning and Changing Through Dynamic Engagement* (San Francisco: Jossey-Bass, 2010).

5. J. Orr, "Sharing Knowledge, Celebrating Identity: War Stories and Community Memory in a Service Culture," in *Collective Remembering: Memory in Society*, ed. D. S. Middleton and D. Edwards (Beverly Hills, CA: Sage, 1990).

6. Ibid.

7. W. Marsalis, *Sweet Swing Blues on the Road: A Year with Wynton Marsalis and His Septet* (New York: W. W. Norton & Co., 1995).

8. P. Berliner, *Thinking in Jazz* (Chicago: University of Chicago Press, 1994).

9. Ibid., 362.

10. Ibid., 382.

11. Ibid., 390.

12. Ibid., 392.

13. W. Wallace, *Michelangelo: The Complete Sculpture, Painting, Architecture* (New York: Beaux Arts Editions, 1998).

14. P. Johnson, *The Renaissance: A Short History* (New York: Modern Library, 2000).

15. See F. Barrett, "Creating Appreciable Learning Cultures," *Organization Dynamics* 24 (1995): 36–49.

16. D. S. Kirschenbaum, "Self-regulation and Sport Psychology: Nurturing an Emerging Symbiosis," *Journal of Sport Psychology* 6 (1984): 159–183.

17. L. Behncke, "Mental Training for Sports: A Brief Review," *Athletic Insight: the Online Journal of Sport Psychology* 6 (March 2004).

18. D. Dorsey, "Positive Deviant," *Fast Company*, November 30, 2000, http://www.fastcompany.com/magazine/41/sternin.html.


*Chapter 3*

1. A. M. Taylor, "Fixing up Ford," *Fortune*, May 12, 2009, http://money.cnn.com/2009/05/11/news/companies/mulally_ford.fortune/index.htm.

2. P. Berliner, *Thinking in Jazz* (Chicago: University of Chicago Press, 1994), 383.

3. Ted Gioia, *The Imperfect Art* (New York: Oxford University Press, 1988).

4. Steven Johnson, *Where Good Ideas Come From* (New York: Riverhead Press, 2010).

5. Ibid., 131–134 (italics in original).

6. Ibid.

7. See http://www.facebook.com/note.php?note_id=17873646561.

8. See http://ecorner.stanford.edu/authorMaterialInfo.html?mid=1528.

9. See http://www.leader-values.com/Content/detail.asp?ContentDetailID=139.

10. E. Hutchins, *Cognition in the Wild* (Cambridge, MA: MIT Press, 1995).

11. A. Tucker and A. Edmondson, "Why Hospitals Don't Learn from Failures," *California Management Review*, January 1, 2003; A. Edmondson, "Strategies for Learning from Failure," *Harvard Business Review* 89, no. 4, April 2012: 48–55.

12. A. Edmondson, *Teaming: How Organizations Learn, Innovate, and Compete in the Knowledge Economy* (San Francisco: Jossey-Bass, 2011), 115–117.

13. M. Gladwell, *Outliers: The Story of Success* (New York: Little, Brown & Co., 2008).

14. A. Edmondson, R. Bohmer, and G. Pisano, "Speeding Up Team Learning," *Harvard Business Review*, October 2001.

15. Ibid.

16. Ibid.

17. M. Bazerman and M. Watkins, *Predictable Surprises* (Boston: Harvard Business School Press, 2004); S. Sitkin, "Learning Through Failure: The Strategy of Small Losses," *Research in Organizational Behavior* 14 (1992): 231–266.

18. R. Ulmer, T. Sellnow, and M. Seeger, *Effective Crisis Communication* (Thousand Oaks, CA: Sage, 2002), 141.

19. Berliner, *Thinking in Jazz*, 41.

20. W. Kahn, "Psychological Conditions of Personal Engagement and Disengagement at Work," *Academy of Management Journal* 33 (1990): 692–724, quote, 694.

21. K. Peplowski, "The Process of Improvisation," *Organization Studies* 9 (1998): 560–562, quote, 561.

22. S. Kierkegaard, *The Present Age* (New York: Harper and Row, 1962) emphasis added.

23. L. Fleming, "Finding the Organizational Sources of Technological Break-throughs: The Story of Hewlett-Packard's Thermal Ink-Jet," *Industrial and Corporate Change* 11 (2002): 1059–1084.

24. Ibid.

25. Ibid.

26. Ibid.

27. Ibid.

28. Ibid.

29. Ibid.

*Chapter 4*

1. In his mega-bestseller *Good to Great*, Jim Collins contends that one of the single-most determining factors in separating great firms from the also-rans is the presence of a transformational leader.

2. D. W. Winnicott, *Playing and Reality* (London: Tavistock, 1971).

3. P. Berliner, *Thinking in Jazz* (Chicago: University of Chicago Press, 1994).

4. M. Wheatley, *Leadership and the New Science* (San Franciso: Berrett-Koehler, 2006); and R. Stacey, *Complexity and Creativity in Organizations* (San Franciso: Berrett-Koehler, 1996).

5. I. Monson, *Saying Something: Jazz Improvisation and Interaction* (Chicago: University of Chicago Press, 1996), 30.

6. Ibid., 29.

7. K. Hawley and N. Means, *Permanent Emergency* (New York: Palgrave Macmillan, 2012), 87.

8. Ibid.

9. K. Weick, "Managing as Improvisation: Lessons from the World of Jazz," Aubrey Fisher Memorial Lectures, University of Utah, October 18, 1990.

10. Dov Frohman and Robert Howard, *Leadership the Hard Way: Why Leadership Can't Be Taught and How You Can Learn It Anyway* (San Francisco: Jossey-Bass, 2008), 7.

11. E. Bernstein and F. J. Barrett, "Strategic Change and the Jazz Mindset: Exploring Practices That Enhance Dynamic Capabilities for Organizational Improvisation," *Research in Organizational Change and Development* 19 (2011): 76.

12. S. Spear, and H. K. Bowen, "Decoding the DNA of the Toyota Production System," *Harvard Business Review* 77, no. 5 (1999): 96–106.

13. Bernstein and Barrett, "Strategic Change and the Jazz Mindset," 55–90.

14. W. Langewiesche, *American Ground: Unbuilding the World Trade Center* (New York: North Point Press, 2002), 19.

15. Ibid., 19.

16. Ibid., 147.

17. Ibid., 12.

18. Ibid., 84.

19. Ibid., 89.

20. Ibid., 112.

21. Ibid., 113.

22. Ibid., 94.

23. Ibid., 118.

24. Ibid.

*Chapter 5*

1. P. Berliner, *Thinking in Jazz* (Chicago: University of Chicago Press, 1994).

2. Ibid., 39.

3. J. V. Wertsch, *Vygotsky and the Social Formation of Mind* (Cambridge, MA: Harvard University Press, 1985).

4. L. Vygotsky, *Thought and Language* (Cambridge, MA: MIT Press, 1986).

5. See http://en.wikipedia.org/wiki/Human_capital.

6. Conversation with author.

7. J. Orr, "Sharing Knowledge, Celebrating Identity: War Stories and Community Memory in a Service Culture," in *Collective Remembering: Memory in Society*, ed. D. S. Middleton and D. Edwards (Beverly Hills, CA: Sage, 1990).

8. Ibid., 42.

9. J. S. Brown and P. Duguid, "Organizational Learning and Communities of Practice: Toward a Unified View of Working, Learning, and Innovation," *Organization Science* 2 (1991): 40–57.

10. J. Lave and E. Wenger, *Situated Learning: Legitimate Peripheral Participation* (Cambridge, UK: Cambridge University Press, 1991).

11. Ibid.

12. D. Thomas and J. S. Brown, "A New Culture of Learning: Cultivating the Imagination for a World of Constant Change," CreateSpace, 2011, 76–77.

13. Ibid.

14. A. Hargadon, *How Breakthroughs Happen* (Boston: Harvard Business School Press, 2003). Here he is citing the *New York Times* obituary section on October 18, 1931.

15. Ibid.

16. W. Isaacson, *Steve Jobs* (New York: Simon and Schuster, 2011), 430.

17. Ibid., 431.

18. Ibid.

19. C. Sunstein, *Going to Extremes* (Oxford, UK: Oxford University Press, 2011).

20. D. Ucbasaran, A. Lockett, and M. Humphreys, "Leading Entrpreneurial Teams: Insights from Jazz," working paper.

21. Ibid.

22. K. Lakhani and J. Panetta, "The Principles of Distributed Innovation," *Innovations: Technology, Governance, Globalization* 2, no. 3 (summer 2007).

23. Ibid., 99.

24. Ibid.

25. See http://www.military.com/features/0,15240,218302,00.html.

## Chapter 6

1. S. Stephenson, "Jazzed about Roy Haynes," *Smithsonian* 34 (2003): 107–114.

2. B. Evans, "Improvisation in Jazz," Liner notes from the CD, *Kind of Blue*, Miles Davis, Columbia/ Legacy, 1997.

3. P. Berliner, *Thinking in Jazz* (Chicago: University of Chicago Press, 1994), 316.

4. Ibid.

5. A. Woolley, C. Habirs, A. Pentland, N. Hashmi, and T. Malone, "Evidence for a Collective Intelligence Factor in the Performance of Human Groups." *Science* 330 (October 2010): 688.

6. J. R. Hackman, *Collaborative Intelligence: Using Teams to Solve Hard Problems* (San Francisco: Berrett-Koehler, 2011), 165. Also see M. Higgins, L. Young, J. Weiner, and S. Wlodarczyk, "Leading Teams of Leaders," *Phi Delta Kappan* 91, no. 4 (2009): 41–45.

7. C. Argyris, *Overcoming Organizational Defenses* (Needham, MA: Allyn-Bacon, 1990).

8. R. M. Kanter, *SuperCorp: How Vanguard Companies Create Innovation, Profits, Growth, and Social Good* (New York: Crown Group, 2009).

9. See https://www.collaborationjam.com/.

10. Ibid.

11. Woolley et al., "Evidence for a Collective Intelligence Factor in the Performance of Human Groups."

12. D. W. Winnicott, *Collected Papers: Through Paediatrics to Psychoanalysis* (London: Tavistock, 1965).

13. R. Kegan and L. Lahey, *How the Way We Talk Can Change the Way We Work: Seven Languages for Transformation* (New York: Jossey Bass, 2001), 52.

14. F. J. Barrett and D. Cooperrider, "Generative Metaphor Intervention: A New Approach to Inter-group Conflict," *Journal of Applied Behavioral Science* 26 (1990): 223–244.

15. See http://www.charlierose.com/shows/2007/08/27/2/a-conversation-with-basketball-professional-steve-nash.

*Chapter* 7

1. See M. Tucker, *The Duke Ellington Reader* (New York: Oxford University Press, 1993). See also D. Ucbasaran, A. Lockett, and M. Humphreys, "Leading Entrepreneurial Teams: Insights from Jazz," working paper.

2. M. Gridley, *Jazz Styles* (Englewood Cliffs, NJ: Prentice-Hall, 1991), 109–110.

3. B. Crow, *Jazz Anecdotes* (New York: Oxford University Press), 281–282.

4. K. Weick, K. Sutcliffe, and D. Obstfeld, "Organizing and the Process of Sensemaking," *Organization Science* 16 (2005): 409–421.

5. D. Boland and F. Collopy, *Managing as Designing* (Chicago: Stanford University Press, 2004).

6. B. Hedberg, P. Nystrom, and W. Starbuck, "Camping on Seesaws: Prescriptions for a Self-Designing Organization," *Administrative Science Quarterly* 21 (March 1976): 41–65.

7. Crow, *Jazz Anecdotes*.

8. Ibid., 281.

9. D. Bailey, *Improvisation* (New York: Da Capo Press, 1992).

10. B. Evans, *The Universal Mind of Bill Evans*, video (New York: Rhapsody Films, 1991).

11. B. Palmer, "The Inner Octaves of Keith Jarrett," *Down Beat*, October 1974.

12. J. Novello, *Contemporary Keyboardist* (Toluea, CA: Source Productions, 1987).

13. D. Carr, *Keith Jarrett* (New York: Da Capo Press, 1991).

14. F. Kaplan, *1959: The Year Everything Changed* (Hoboken NJ: Wiley and Sons, 2009).

15. C. Dawson, *Lexus: The Relentless Pursuit: How Toyota Motor Went From "0-60" in the Global Luxury Car Market* (Hoboken, NJ: Wiley, 2004).

16. A. Taylor III and W. E. Sheeline, "Here Come Japan's New Luxury Cars: First Out of the Gate, Toyota's Lexus Is as Good as, or Better Than, More Expensive German Makes. But Will American Buyers Forgo Teutonic Mystique?" *Fortune*, August 14, 1989.

17. Dawson, *Lexus: The Relentless Pursuit*, 40.

18. Ibid., xix.

19. Ibid.

20. E. Bernstein and F. J. Barrett, "Strategic Change and the Jazz Mindset: Exploring Practices That Enhance Dynamic Capabilities for Organizational Improvisation," *Research in Organizational Change and Development* 19 (2011): 55–90.

21. Ibid.


*Chapter 8*

1. A. Carr, "The Most Important Leadership Quality for CEO's Creativity," *Fast Company*, May 18, 2010. Available at http://www.fastcompany.com/1648943/creativity-the-most-important-leadership-quality-for-ceos-study.

2. W. Duggan, *Napoleon's Glance: The Secret of Strategy* (New York: Nation Books, 2003).

3. P. Senge, *The Fifth Discipline* (New York: Doubleday, 1990).

4. See C. Hampden-Turner, *Charting the Corporate Mind* (New York: Free Press, 1990).

5. Arie de Geus, "Planning as Learning," *Harvard Business Review* 66, no. 2 (1998): 70–74.

6. N. Katz, "Sports Teams as a Model for Workplace Teams: Lessons and Liabilities," *Academy of Management Executive* vol. 15, no. 3 (2001): 56–67.

7. A. L. Delbecq, A. H. Van de Ven, and D. Gustafson, *Group Techniques for Program Planning* (Glenview, IL: Scott-Foresman, 1975).

8. Ibid.

9. E. Eisenberg, "Jamming: Transcendence Through Organizing," *Communication Research* 17, no. 2, (April 1990): 139–164; and M. Csikszentmihalyi, *Flow: The Psychology of Optimal Experience* (New York: Harper, 1990).

10. R. E. Quinn, *Beyond Rational Management: Mastering the Paradoxes and Competing Demands of High Performance* (San Fransisco: Jossey-Bass, 1988).

11. See P. Meyers, *From Workspace to Playspace* (San Francisco: Jossey-Bass, 2010).

12. S. Johnson, *Where Good Ideas Come From* (New York: Riverhead, 2011).

13. W. Isaacson, *Steve Jobs* (New York: Simon and Schuster, 2011), 431.

14. E. Von Hippel, *Democratizing Innovation* (Cambridge, MA: MIT Press, 2005).

15. Ibid.

16. C. Argyris, "Double Loop Learning in Organizations," *Harvard Business Review* 55, no. 5 (1977): 115–125; and A. C. Edmondson, "Strategies for Learning from Failure," *Harvard Business Review* 89, no. 4 (April 2012): 48–55.

17. D. L. Cooperrider and S. Srivastva, "Appreciative Inquiry into Organizational Life." In W. A. Pasmore and R. W. Woodman (eds.) *Research in Organizational Change and Development,* vol. 1 (Greenwich, CT: JAI Press, 1987), 129–169. See also F. J. Barrett and D. Cooperrider, "Generative Metaphor Intervention: A New Approach to Inter-group Conflict," *Journal of Applied Behavioral Science* 26 (1990): 223–244.

# INDEX

accompanying a solo improvisation ("comping"), 122–123, 174–175
active followership, 130–134
Adderly, Cannonball, 146, 150
advancing improvisation
  CEOs' agreement on value of innovation, 161–162
  characteristics of improvising organizations, 182–183
  goal of organizations to "hit the groove," 162–163
  toolkit for (see improvisation toolkit)
aesthetic of imperfection, 44–46
affirmative competence
  approaching leadership tasks as experiments, 163–165
  benefit of a mind-set that maximizes opportunities, 36–37
  Bezos's response to Unbox failure, 21–22
  bias towards positivity, 24
  characteristics of improvisational leaders, 39
  expanding the vocabulary of "yes," 169–171
  Herman Miller's creative response to a series of challenges, 22–24
  Michelangelo's approach to carving David, 35–36
  positive expectations and, 37–39
  positive outcome from saying "yes to the mess" example, 29–30
  reality of indeterminate tasks in business, 26–27
  retrospective playing example, 27–29
Amazon.com, 21–22

American Ground (Langewiesche), 85
Apple, 50, 120
apprenticeship model of education, 104
Arendt, Hannah, 46
attentive listening, 125

banking concept of learning, 13, 98
Baum, Dan, 18
Bazerman, Max, 54
bebop, 143
Bernhart, Milt, 139
Bernstein, Ethan, 80, 81–82, 155
Bezos, Jeff, 21–22
bias toward positivity, 24
Boland, Richard, 138
BP (British Petroleum), 1–2, 3, 10
bricolage, 25–26
Bridge, The (recording), 15–16
British Airways, 152
Brown, John Seely, 104, 105
Brown, Ray, 62
Burton, Mike, 86. See also World Trade Center cleanup

Carter, Ron, 146
Chambers, Paul, 145
Chaos (Gleick), 74
Chardack, William, 48
Christensen, Clayton, 140
Cleaver, Liam, 127–128
Cobb, Jimmy, 145
Coleridge, Samuel Taylor, 11
collaboration

followership and, 126, 127–128
keeping it loose and informal,
  113–116
learning through, 104–105
mutual reliance and, 125
working environment and, 110
collective intelligence, 126, 129–130
Collins, Jim, 68, 120
Coltrane, John, 122, 142, 145,
  146–147
communities of practice, 95–97,
  104–105
competence, affirmative. *See* affirmative
  competence
competency trap
  breaking out of, 141–143
  using provocative competence to
    beat, 143–147
"comping" in an organization,
  122–123, 174–175
complexity theory, 70–73
Cooperrider, David, 132
Cowley, Neil, 112
creative community, 116–117
creativity. *See* jam sessions
crowdsourcing, 113–116

DARPA (Defense Advanced Research
  Project Agency), 115–116
Davis, Miles
  ability to "hit the groove," 34
  acceptance of errors, 43
  competency trap avoidance
    techniques, 142–143, 144
  generous listening and, 121–122
  maximizing of diversity, 112
  provocative competence of,
    147–150
Davis, Richard, 125
Deepwater Horizon oil rig, 1–2, 3
Defense Advanced Research Project
  Agency (DARPA), 115–116
de Forest, Lee, 47
de Geus, Arie, 166

*Democracy and Education* (Dewey),
  106–107
De Niro, Robert, 67
Dewey, John, 106–107
Donald, Dave, 63
Drucker, Peter, 2
Duguid, Paul, 104

eBay, 153
Edison, Thomas, 108, 109
Edmondson, Amy, 52, 54
egocentric passion, 127
Ellington, Duke, 135–137, 139, 147
Evans, Bill, 8, 62, 113, 121, 142,
  145, 146

Fields, Mark, 41
"Flamenco Sketches" (song), 146
Flanagan, Tommy, 32
Fleming, Lee, 62–63, 64
followership
  accepting both a soloing and
    supporting mind-set,
    126–128
  attentive listening's role in enabling
    performance, 125
  collaborative intelligence studies
    and, 126
  "comping" in an organization,
    122–123
  creating a culture of noble
    followership, 174–175
  cult of the leader, 119–121
  egocentric passion and, 127
  factors that make groups smart,
    129–130
  generous listening, 121–122
  giving everyone a chance to solo,
    173–174
  "holding environment" and active
    followership, 130–132,
    133–134

IBM's online collaborative
discussion, 127–128
other-centric compassion and, 127
supportive role of good followership, 132–134
value in taking turns leading and
following, 123–125
Ford Motor Company, 41–42
Freire, Paulo, 12, 98
Friedman, Don, 44
Frohman, Dov, 77
Fuller, Curtis, 96
FunSaver camera, 76–77

GE (General Electric), 13
gender composition of a group and
collective intelligence, 130
generous listening, 121–122
Getz, Stan, 62
Giant Manufacturing Company,
155–158
Gioia, Ted, 10, 25, 44
Gladwell, Malcom, 54
Gleick, James, 74
GNU Project, 79
Good to Great (Collins), 68, 120
Google, 50
Gore, Bill, 151–152
Granz, Norman, 55
Greatbatch, Wilson, 47–48
Gridley, Mark, 8, 136
Grove, Andy, 16–17
guided autonomy, 77–79

Habitat Jam at IBM, 128
Hackman, Richard, 126
Hagan, Arthur E., 4
Hancock, Herbie, 142, 146
Hanna, Roland, 125
Hargadon, Andrew, 108, 109
Hawley, Kip, 74–75
Haynes, Roy, 121
Hayward, Tony, 2, 10

Herman Miller, 22
Hersch, Fred, 34
Hewlett-Packard, 62–65
Holden, Ken, 88
"holding environment," 130–132,
133–134
hot-wash sessions, 167
Howard, Robert, 77
Hughes, Chris, 17–18

IBM, 127–128
IDEO, 65, 126
Immelt, Jeffrey, 13
improvisation. See advancing improvisation; improvisation toolkit; jazz
improvisation
"Improvisation as a Mindset for
Organizational Performance"
(Weick), 2
improvisation toolkit
allowing jam sessions, 178–179
approaching leadership tasks as
experiments, 163–165
boosting information processing,
165–167
celebrating "comping" to create a
culture of noble followership,
174–175
creating minimal structures that
maximize autonomy,
175–176
cultivating provocative competence,
179–181
deliberately breaking routines,
167–169
encouraging serious play and less
control, 177–178
expanding the vocabulary of "yes,"
169–171
giving everyone a chance to solo,
173–174
learning from failure, 171–173
inclusive involvement and turn taking
in groups, 129–130

innovation
    CEOs' agreement on value of inno-
        vation, 161–162
    developed through interactions,
        108–110
    guided autonomy's role in, 77–79
    Innovation Jam at IBM, 127–128
    parallels to jazz improvisation, 8–10
Innovation Jam at IBM, 127–128
Intel, 16–17
Isaacson, Walter, 109–110

jam sessions
    allowing, 178–179
    cognition and social processes and,
        97–99
    communities of practice and, 95–97,
        104–105
    creative community example,
        116–117
    crowdsourcing's basis in loose
        and informal collaboration,
        113–116
    danger of losing creativity due
        to homogeneity of a group,
        111–113
    innovations developed through
        interactions, 108–110
    learning as doing and, 103–104
    learning through active doing,
        106–107
    mistake of a focus on individualism
        in invention, 110–111
    opportunities lost through an
        overreliance on structured
        learning, 100–101
    spontaneous nature of, 102–103
    as a vehicle for learning and creativ-
        ity, 93–95, 178–179
Jarrett, Keith, 14, 62, 142, 143
jazz improvisation
    applicability of learning jazz to learn-
        ing business management, 4–6
    bricolage-like qualities, 25–26

    characteristics of great jazz players, 6
    complexity theory applied to jazz
        bands, 71–73
    complex system's comfort with
        chaos, 67–68
    deliberately breaking routines,
        167–169
    emergent system benefits, 18
    establishing a groove, 33–35
    fundamentals of, 8
    goal of improvisation, 7
    how jazz players learn to improvise, 7
    learning through experimentation,
        11–12
    military-based example of improvi-
        sation, 17–18
    parallels to entrepreneurship and
        innovation, 8–10
    quality of continual negotiation,
        31–33
    retrospective nature of, 25
    routines versus improv, 14–17
    value in taking turns leading and
        following, 124–125
    World Trade Center cleanup paral-
        lels to, 91–92
jazz musicians
    acceptance of errors, 43–44
    competency trap avoidance,
        141–143
    imperative of diversity, 65
    letting go of deliberation and
        control, 61–62
Jobs, Steve, 9, 109–110, 120, 178
Johnson, Mary Lou, 58–60
Johnson, Paul, 36
Johnson, Steven, 47, 178
Jones, Sean, 112

Kahn, William, 60
Kaplan, Fred, 146–147
Katz, Nancy, 166–167
Keats, John, 11
Kegan, Robert, 131

Kelley, David, 65
Kelly, Wynton, 113
Khurana, Rakesh, 120
Kierkegaard, Søren, 23, 61–62
Kind of Blue (recording), 144–145, 148–149
Kleiner Perkins Caufield & Byers, 50
knowledge transfer through social interaction, 98–99
Kodak, 76–77
Komisar, Randy, 50
Konitz, Lee, 32, 125

Lacy, Steve, 8
Lakhani, Karim, 114
Langewiesche, William, 85, 86
Lave, Jean, 104
leadership
    allowing jam sessions, 179
    approaching leadership tasks as experiments, 163–165
    celebrating "comping" to create a culture of noble followership, 174–175
    characteristics of improvisational leaders, 39
    creating minimal structures that maximize autonomy, 176
    cultivating provocative competence, 180–181
    cult of the leader, 119–121
    deliberately breaking routines, 169
    design mind-set approach to, 137–138
    Ellington's leadership approach, 135–137, 139
    expanding the vocabulary of "yes," 171
    giving everyone a chance to solo, 174
    learning from failure, 171–173
    as provocative competence (see provocative competence)
    value in taking turns leading and following, 123–125
Leadership the Hard Way (Frohman and Howard), 77
learning
    applicability of learning jazz to learning business management, 4–6
    banking concept of learning, 13, 98
    from failure, 171–173
    hierarchical impediments to, 54
    how jazz players learn to improvise, 7
    jam sessions as a vehicle for, 93–95, 178–179
    Marsalis's openness to, 56–57
    overreliance on structured learning, 100–101
    through active doing in jam sessions, 103–104, 106–107
    through collaboration, 104–105
    through experimentation, 11–12
    treating errors as learning opportunities, 51–53
learning through active doing, 106–107
LEGO Mindstorms, 178–179
Lévi-Strauss, Claude, 25
Lewis, Ted, 57–60
Linux, 79, 114–115
Little, Brooker, 44
Lo, Tony, 155–158

Marsalis, Ellis, 56–57
Marsalis, Wynton, 31, 56–57
Mayer, Marissa, 50
McBee, Cecil, 72
McDonough, William, 22
McVicker, Noah and Joseph, 49
Meyer, John, 63, 64
Michelangelo and David, 35–36
Microsoft, 50
Mingus, Charles, 67, 79, 137

minimal structure, maximal autonomy
   complex adaptive systems'
      advantages, 68–69
   complexity theory applied to jazz
      bands, 71–73
   complexity theory applied to
      organizations, 70–71
   components of minimal structure,
      73–75
   coordination through minimal
      structure example (*see* World
      Trade Center cleanup)
   creating, 175–176
   freedom and vigilance in
      improvisation, 70
   guided autonomy and group
      dynamics, 82–85
   guided autonomy's role in
      innovation, 77–79
   jazz improvisation's comfort with
      chaos, 67–68
   loose coupling and dynamic
      capability, 79–82
   organizational equivalent of
      minimal structure, 75–76
   organizational routes to encouraging
      improvisation, 76–77
   organizational stories and myths'
      roles in eliciting creative
      responses, 76
   success's basis in freedom and
      vigilance, 70
   system robustness improved by
      accepting errors, 75
Mulally, Alan, 41

Napoleon, 164
Nash, Steve, 133
Naval Postgraduate School,
   57–58, 100
Network Challenge from DARPA,
   116
9/11 cleanup. *See* World Trade Center
   cleanup

Nordstrom, 45–46
Oaxley, Tony, 142
Omidyar, Pierre, 153
Omni Hotel experiment, 82–85
Omron, 80–81
*Only the Paranoid Survive* (Grove),
   16–17
open-source software, 79, 113–116
Orr, Julian, 27
other-centric compassion, 127
*Outliers* (Gladwell), 54

pacemaker invention, 47–49
Palmisano, Sam, 127
Panetta, Jill, 114
Parker, Charlie, 94–95
Parks, Jay, 168
Peplowski, Ken, 28, 61, 93, 129–130
performing and experimenting
      simultaneously
   allowing an aesthetic of
      imperfection within an
      organization, 44–46
   boosting information processing,
      165–167
   capitalizing on constructive failure,
      49–51, 171–173
   encouraging serious play and less
      control, 177–178
   hierarchical impediments to
      learning, 54
   imperative of diversity of employee
      backgrounds, 65
   inventive process's success at HP,
      62–65
   jazz musicians' acceptance of errors,
      43–44
   jazz musicians' letting go of
      deliberation and control, 61–62
   Marsalis's openness to learning,
      56–57
   Mulally's encouragement of honesty
      at Ford, 41–42
   pacemaker invention story, 47–49

Peterson's commitment to
    perfection, 55–56
Play-Doh invention story, 49
Rollins's willingness to
    experiment, 56
standard characterization of the
    competent manager, 60
taking advantages of errors, 46–47
treating errors as learning
    opportunities, 51–53
value in a culture and leadership
    that allows risk taking, 57–60
value in a team culture that tolerates
    errors, 42, 53–55
*Permanent Emergency* (Hawley), 74
Persip, Charlie, 69
Peterson, Oscar, 13–14, 55–56
Peterson, Ralph, 73
planning
    applicability of learning jazz to
        learning business management,
        4–6
    business school stressing of routines,
        12–13
    deliberately breaking routines,
        167–169
    reality of unexpected situations, 1–3
Play-Doh, 49
provocative competence
    barriers to, 152–153
    beating the competency trap
        example, 143–147
    competency trap and, 140–143
    creating positive change by nurturing
        double vision, 150–152
    cultivating, 179–181
    deconstructing, 147–150
    design mind-set approach to
        leadership, 137–138
    Ellington's leadership approach,
        135–137, 139, 147
    explained, 139–140
    Giant's women-only bike store
        genesis and realization,
        155–158

setting the bar high at Toyota, 154
transcending conventional practices,
    158–159

Quinn, James Brian, 51, 177

Roach, Max, 33
Roadway Trucking, 183
Rollins, Sonny, 14, 15–16, 56

Sakuta, Hisao, 80
Sanger, Larry, 78
"scaffolding," 97
Scott, Ronnie, 14
*Searching for a Corporate Savior*
    (Khurana), 120
Seeger, Matthew, 55
Sellnow, Timothy, 55
Senge, Peter, 166
Shorter, Wayne, 146
Shula, Don, 166
Simon, Herbert, 138
Sitkin, Sim, 54
*Situated Learning* (Lave and
    Wegner), 104
Snook, Scott, 168
social sensitivity and collective
    intelligence, 129
Sony, 152
"So What?" (song), 145
*Speeding Up Learning*
    (Edmondson), 54
Stacey, Ralph, 70
Stallman, Richard, 79
Sternin, Jerry, 38–39
Sunstein, Cass, 111

Terry, Clark, 139
Threadless, 116–117
Tizol, Juan, 137
TopCoder, 115

Torvalds, Linus, 79, 114
Toyoda, Eiji, 153–154
Toyota, 81–82, 153–154
Tu, Bonnie, 157–158
Turrentine, Tommy, 7
Tyner, McCoy, 121

Ulmer, Robert, 55
Unbox, 21–22

ValuesJam at IBM, 127–128
Vaught, John, 63, 64
Vygotsky, Lev, 97

Wales, Jimmy, 78
Watkins, Michael, 54
Weick, Karl, 2, 6, 10, 75
Wenger, Etienne, 104
Wheatley, Meg, 70
Wikipedia, 78, 79, 113
Williams, Buster, 34
Williams, Cootie (Charles Melvin), 136

Williams, Tony, 143, 146
Winnicott, Donald, 69, 131
W. L. Gore and Associates, 151
Woolley, Anita, 126
World Trade Center cleanup
    ad hoc team assembly by Burton,
        87–88
    four-pile arrangement genesis,
        89–90
    hazardous materials danger, 85–86
    lack of an official order to proceed,
        90
    loyalty conflicts, 86
    minimal structure created by
        scheduled meetings, 88–89
    parallels to jazz improvisation,
        91–92
    spontaneous arrival of workers, 88
    success of, 86

Xerox, 103

zone of proximal development, 97

# ABOUT THE AUTHOR

**Frank J. Barrett** is Professor of Management and Global Public Policy in the Graduate School of Business and Public Policy at the Naval Postgraduate School in Monterey, California. From 2008–2010 he was a Visiting Scholar at Harvard Business School and also at Harvard Law School's Program on Negotiation. He held the Boer & Croon Chair of Change Management at Tilburg University (Netherlands) and has served on the faculties of Katholieke University of Leuven (Belgium), Penn State University's Behrend College, Case Western Reserve University, Fielding Graduate University, and Benedictine University.

He holds a BA in Government and International Relations and an MA in English from the University of Notre Dame and a PhD in Organizational Behavior from Case Western Reserve University.

Frank has served as a consultant to numerous organizations, including Harvard University, Boeing, the US Navy, Ford Motor Manufacturing Division, Ford Motor Information Strategy Group, Bell South, Granite Construction, Glaxo Wellcome, General Electric, British Petroleum, Nokia, Johnson & Johnson, PricewaterhouseCoopers, the BBC, the Council of Great Lakes Governors, Omni Hotels, the Cleveland Clinic Foundation, and University Hospitals of Cleveland.

Frank has written and lectured widely on social constructionism, appreciative inquiry, organizational change, jazz improvisation, and organizational learning. He is coauthor, with Ron Fry, of *Appreciative Inquiry: A Positive Approach to Building Cooperative Capacity*. He has published articles on metaphor, masculinity, improvisation, organizational change, and organizational development in the *Journal of Applied Behavioral Science*; *Human Relations*; *Organization Science*; and *Organizational Dynamics*, as well as numerous book chapters. He wrote "Generative Metaphor Intervention: A New Approach to Intergroup

Conflict" (with David Cooperrider), which won the award for best paper from the Organization Development and Change Division of the Academy of Management in 1988. He won the best paper award again in 2003 for "Planning on Spontaneity: Lessons from Jazz for a Democratic Theory of Change," which he coauthored with Mary Jo Hatch. He is coeditor of *Appreciative Inquiry and Organizational Transformation*.

Frank is an active jazz pianist. In addition to leading his own trios and quartets, he has traveled extensively in the United States, England, and Mexico with the Tommy Dorsey Orchestra.